HONEYMOON FOR LIFE

HONEYMOON

FOR LIFE

Joanna Woolfolk

STEIN AND DAY / *Publishers* / New York

First published in 1979
Copyright © 1979 by Joanna Woolfolk
All rights reserved
Designed by Karen Bernath
Printed in the United States of America
Stein and Day/*Publishers*/Scarborough House,
Briarcliff Manor, N.Y. 10510

Library of Congress Cataloging in Publication Data

Woolfolk, Joanna.
  Honeymoon for life.

  1. Marriage.   2. Family.   3. Sex in marriage.
4. Love.   I. Title.
HQ734.W938   301.42'7   77-15966
ISBN 0-8128-2443-1

To Bill,
my own honeymooner
for life

Contents

HONEYMOON
FOR
LIFE

Epilog

An epilog is something added after the conclusion of a work.

What is an epilog doing here on page 1?

Because I hope that reading this book will lead you to the conclusion of something: your humdrum marriage. Psychologists delve into the reasons people fall in love and marry, and into the reasons people fall out of love and divorce. But very few appear to be as interested in a more prevalent problem: a marriage that seems to have gone stale around the edges, a relationship that isn't as much fun as it used to be, a romance that once bloomed like the rose and now is starting, just starting, to wither.

Honeymoon for Life is written for women who find themselves in just that situation. Of course, husbands are equally important in the making of a happy marriage. But I am a woman and I write more easily from a woman's viewpoint. It doesn't matter from which angle a problem is approached, as long as it is solved.

I won't pretend to you that there is an easy answer to the question of how to be eternally happy in marriage. "For every difficult problem," H. L. Mencken said, "there is an answer that is short, simple—and wrong."

But I can promise you that the problem of restoring to your marriage some of its lost vitality is neither difficult nor complex. You will find no involved explanations here, no delving into psychological profundities. Everything in these pages is taken from my own experience, the experience of my friends, and the experiences of the more than 65 "honeymooners for life" I interviewed.

I'm not sure how many of their insights will sound new to you. There is nothing really new under the sun, but there *is* a new way of looking at it. I can't give anyone a new pair of eyes. But I can help you to use the eyesight you already have—to see what's been there all the time, to perceive what you may feel you've known all along.

Happiness in marriage can't be taught, but it can be *learned*. When the excitement and glamor of the honeymoon have faded, marriage does not have to become a hearse that carries happiness to its grave. Being happy *and* married is a natural condition. I'll grant there seem to be a lot of exceptions to that statement, but that's like saying there is a lot of illness in the world. It doesn't change the fact that being healthy is a natural condition. Just as you can recover good health, you can recover happiness in marriage. You can infuse a relationship that's been threatening to become dull and dreary with fresh discovery and excitement and sexy fun.

I am presuming, of course, that you *want* to stay with your marriage and to make it better. I have not written this book for those who are deeply unhappy in marriage. This book is for those whose marriages have a lot going for them but who still want something extra. A marriage that is navigating in shallow water does not have to end up on the rocks.

When you finish reading *Honeymoon for Life*, no earthquake will have happened. No hurricane. But you will have learned a lot about how to recapture that sexy, sensual time when you and your husband delighted in each other, paid devoted attention to each other, were turned-on to each other.

Oscar Wilde said, "When one is in love, one always begins by deceiving oneself, and one always ends by deceiving others. That is what the world calls romance."

That doesn't have to be so. Among the happily married honeymooners-for-life that I interviewed for this book, there were none who proclaimed their marriage to be a state of rapture, unadulterated and *wow*, the be-all and end-all of existence. That kind of idyllic human relationship probably doesn't exist. It ended when the first snake slithered into Eden and everyone stopped being perfect. Human nature is too marvelously varied and unpredictable, and living is so full of little crises, unfulfilled needs, fears, and anxieties, that it's hard to imagine how people can avoid having moments of melancholy or discontent.

However, it *is* perfectly possible to avoid the apathy-verging-on-boredom that characterizes too many marriages, the kind that seem to be lit with a 40-watt bulb. Most couples don't suffer from the severe incompatibility that turns marriage into a close encounter of the worst kind. But that is far from true happiness. "There are many good marriages, but few delightful ones," a wit once observed. And a delightful marriage so far surpasses a "good" marriage that it is strictly no contest.

You have a right to a delightful marriage. I hope in this book to provide practical guidelines on how to achieve it. You don't have to spend months or years on a psychoanalyst's couch, study Zen or Yoga, or smoke exotic Indian herbs. In revitalizing a relationship, there are no complicated formulas, no hidden erogenous zones you touch to make joy pop out. You needn't become Totally Submissive, and, on the other hand, if you think a day without Anita Bryant is like a month of sunshine, you won't have to change your mind.

When you picked up this book, you took an important step toward removing the monotony from monogamy because you began looking for an answer. Think of all the people who were hit on the head by a falling apple (before Isaac Newton was) and who never

Epilog

wondered why. You were hit on the head by the apple of discontent and you did begin to wonder why.

From now on, we'll look for answers together.

It's time to stop writing this introduction, and to begin.

PART I

DON'T BE HIS WIFE, BE HIS LOVER

Speaking Personally

I fell in love with my husband before I met him.

At the time, I was working as assistant to the chief editor of a large book publishing firm. The job paid well. My boss, Lee Barker, was a handsome 60-year-old man married to an absolutely gorgeous woman. I envied Lee and Adeline. I pictured myself as living in an elegant New York City cooperative apartment like theirs, dining out at fabulous restaurants, going to the theater, having a private box at Shea Stadium to watch the Mets, giving lavish parties to entertain famous authors, and traveling to the Caribbean on frequent holidays—each time to a different island.

One day Mr. Barker told me about a novel written by a friend who had been a magazine publisher and was currently the story editor for the popular and prestigious television drama, "The Defenders." Mr.

Barker asked me to read the manuscript and tell him what I thought.

That night I was so caught up in reading that I hardly slept. I finished the manuscript at 4:00 A.M. Hours later, while taking a shower, I thought of a blurb for the book jacket. Lee Barker liked it, and passed it along to the author.

The next mail brought a very funny letter in which the author said the mere thought of me in the shower had so unmanned him that he couldn't resist accepting my suggestion. But he foresaw a problem. Every time he saw the jacket blurb, would he be reminded of me in the shower?

"Is he married?" I asked Lee Barker.

"Very," I was told.

Well, that was that. We exchanged a few notes in the course of business—he was amusing, considerate, articulate, and charming.

But married.

One day the author came into the office to talk over his book with Lee Barker. He was tall, good looking, as charming and even more amusing in person than in correspondence. Exactly the sort of man I had in mind to share that elegant New York cooperative apartment.

I pushed the thought firmly aside. I've always believed that when you see trouble coming down the street you should jump up on the curb and let it pass by.

Then Lee Barker suggested that I join the two of

them for lunch and contribute any ideas I might have for promoting and publishing the novel. At lunch, I had the distinct impression that Bill—we were on a first-name basis—was interested in me, even though he talked most of the time to Lee Barker. The moment I took out a cigarette he was ready with a match, guarding the flame for me in his cupped hands. When he discovered that I drank only wine, he ordered a bottle of imported French champagne for our table. Nothing helps along an occasion like the Pied Piper of Heidseck.

While I drank champagne—feeling frivolous and indulged and somehow more beautiful—a nagging thought returned: *Forget it. He's married.*

A few days later Bill called the office to ask if Lee Barker could have lunch with him to discuss plans for promoting his book. Unfortunately, Mr. Barker was away from the office at an editorial conference. Bill's next question: Will *you* have lunch with me?

It's business, I thought, and lunch certainly can't do any harm.

Not only was Bill a fascinating luncheon companion, but he managed to convey the impression—eloquently, though not in words—that I was the most fascinating luncheon companion *he'd* ever known.

I learned that, far from being "very" married, he was in the process of separating from his wife. For several years they had been among the millions of spiritually, mentally, and physically divorced couples who are still legally married. I began to feel like someone in a canoe being pulled toward a waterfall.

That evening Bill called me at my apartment in Greenwich Village. He asked me to dinner.

When I accepted, I knew there was no turning back.

It's Wonderful Anywhere

Reader, I married him.

Shortly afterward, Bill's novel having been chosen by two book clubs, he left his job as a television story editor for "The Defenders" to become a full-time novelist.

And we promptly set off on a two-year tour. "Have typewriter, will travel" was Bill's motto; as long as he had a corner in which to write, we could live anywhere. We went to London and Paris and Venice, to Rome and Ireland. We lived in Barbados and on Sanibel Island on the Gulf Coast of Florida. We spent summers at a boathouse converted into a picturesque cottage right on the edge of Pleasant Bay in Cape Cod.

I could not imagine a more perfect life. We were having what amounted to a two-year honeymoon.

Bill and I spent every hour of every day together. Even when he wasn't with me, I could hear his typewriter in an adjoining room. I edited and typed his manuscripts; I learned to cook. I had always thought of myself as the kind who couldn't break an egg without ruining an omelet, but I took such pleasure in pleasing Bill that I became a gourmet cook. I found myself walking around and saying to myself—literally saying it— "The world is so full of a number of things, I think we should all be as happy as kings!"

I never thought our idyll would have to end. But, of course, it did. We'd been traveling for two years, taking practically everything we owned along with us. That included correspondence, books, income tax records, piles of manuscripts, as well as clothing and personal belongings. Whenever we arrived in a new city we had to take two taxis, one just to carry our extra luggage. And we stayed in furnished places with borrowed dishes, towels, hardly anything to call our own. Our lives were becoming too complicated. It was time to settle down.

I had no idea how far "down" was.

Heartfall

We settled in Los Angeles. We rented a lovely garden apartment with all the amenities of Southern California living, from Olympic swimming pool and jacuzzi to gymnasium, from ping pong to billiards. We renewed old friendships, began new ones. I loved to entertain, and we had parties once or twice a week. We attended preview screenings of all the important new movies at the Writers Guild theater.

We still enjoyed each other's company, and I still thought Bill the most amusing, attractive man in the world. I was proud to have him as an escort. He was writing novels which were well received. He was turning down highly lucrative television offers, partly because it would mean being away from me much of the time. He could write novels on a less demanding schedule, and we could be together.

Together! I wanted that, but the kind of together-ness I wanted included all the enchantment of our first years. Was I naive to expect so much? Perhaps it was impossible to sustain happiness at that level.

But why not? I wondered. *Why* did life have to settle into a routine? Why couldn't I always experience that marvelous butterflies-in-the-stomach feeling I used to have when I saw Bill coming toward me on the street? It wasn't fair to have so much, then have to settle for less.

I couldn't define what was going wrong, but something definitely was.

With sudden dread, I foresaw that we might eventually become like all those other married couples who acted as if their lives were only bed and bored. Many times I had looked at such people and found it hard to imagine what they saw in each other in the beginning. What harps had sung in the air? What bells had started to ring?

One day, Bill and I were returning from a movie preview. We were discussing the plot and the actors, as was our habit. I said the actress in the movie, a newcomer, couldn't act and wasn't all that good look-ing, so she certainly didn't have a future. Bill dis-agreed.

"She's going to be a star," he told me. "She's got the one ingredient men look for in a woman."

"What's that?" I asked, dimly aware that I might be receiving a covert message.

"Sensuality," he said. "A woman without sensuality might as well be an ice statue for all the appeal she has to most men."

Was he trying to tell me I *wasn't* "sensual"? I'd been told that I was quite attractive. Lee Barker had put up with plenty of office jokes about his having such a sexy assistant. And until now, Bill had never hinted that I was not more than appealing to him in a physical way. Quite the opposite. He was always so quick with compliments, so eager for. . . .

Wait!

Real Life and Reel Life

When was the last time he had paid me that kind of compliment? He used to joke about my sultry voice on the telephone ("It's a wonder men don't come crawling over the wire to you"), about how he liked to walk half a block behind me on the street sometimes just so he could see how men turned to look at me after I'd passed by. ("And I don't blame them a bit!") When was the last time he had really *prepared* for a romantic evening?

Not for months.

At this point in my reasoning I was more than a little defensive. Was he actually comparing me with women on a motion picture screen? He ought to know how wide was the gulf between real and reel life.

And why was it just up to me to be "sensual"? That kind of criticism cuts both ways. Wasn't he equally responsible if our love life had become settled, predictable, unexciting? We were still able to give each other pleasure, like actors who can step into a familiar role without much rehearsal and still give a satisfactory performance. But was that enough?

Kind But Evasive

I waited a reasonable time, until one night when we were comfortably at home watching *Casablanca* for the twelfth time: "Isn't Ingrid Bergman beautiful?" I asked with as much casualness as I could muster.

"She certainly is."

"Is *she* sensual?"

"You bet!"

The time had come. My sensitive soul was asking to be pierced—like a boil. "Am I?"

"You aren't worrying about it, are you?"

"Well . . . a little."

His tone was reassuring. "That's silly."

Was he trying to be kind? Or evasive?

"You haven't answered my question," I said.

"It's hard to answer. We've been married quite a while, darling. I don't think of you in that way. Let's watch the picture."

So it *was* serious.

Eyes To See

I admit that I was stunned. But I wasn't going to be one of those wives who, when confronted by a problem, do nothing about it. Being a passive spectator never has appealed to me, and I certainly had no intention of being passive about my marriage!

On the other hand, I was not going to change into someone else—nor pretend to. God forbid that I'd ever become one of those Totally Fascinating Doormats, the desperate women who become submissive dunces just to keep their husbands from stomping on them. There had to be a better way. All I needed was the will to find it.

Dailiness

I began by going to the library. I read all the books in the card catalog that seemed to have anything to say about the creeping ennui of marriage.

I discovered that, although the problem was universally recognized, no one seemed to know what to do about it. "The trouble with marriage is its *dailiness*," declared Arnold Bennett, the famous English author. Like the others, he had no solutions to offer.

So I talked to friends, acquaintances, even comparative strangers who seemed to have licked the problem of how to stay happy though married. I didn't walk up to them and say, "My husband and I are two lovers in a slowly sinking gondola. Do you happen to have a bailing bucket?" I told them I was doing research for a book my husband was writing on successful marriages. Many people I interviewed then will learn here for the first time that they were being conned. But it was in a good cause, and I hope they'll understand and forgive.

A Dramatic Change

Gradually, from everything I read and everyone I talked to, I began to diagnose the disease that ate away at the heart of most marriages. It was the absence of sensuality—a lack of the mutual gratification of the senses, which is the uniting power in marriage. My husband was not wrong, although he had not bothered to define what he meant. Sensuality involves the whole person, not just the genitals. Sensualness pervades a relationship, and without it, true intimacy—true delight in the presence of another—is unlikely.

I intend to share what I've learned about sensuality. In a surprisingly short amount of time, you too can do a great deal to change your weary, stale, flat, and unprofitable marriage into what it was before the wheels started to run down. You can relearn the secret of enchantment and wonder.

You may not be able to go back to the beginning, when all the world was young. But what you had then has not been truly lost. Love is always waiting to be rediscovered.

I can't improve on what my husband wrote at the end of one of his novels (*Maggie: A Love Story*).

> When you have loved deeply, when you have been able truly to give yourself, something is given back to you. You hold forever in your heart the secret of what it means to be alive.

Unlocking Your Sensuality— and His

"Women are more sensitive to unspoken messages than men," says Dr. Joyce Brothers.

Indeed, women do have a better emotional radar. Tones of voice, the wordless signals of body language, the hidden meanings to be read in facial expressions are all clues for the sensitive female. And we begin to use our radar detection early in life.

I remember that when I was about ten, I used to love to go to the dentist because he thought I was pretty. On the morning of my dentist appointment, I made sure my mother arranged my long dark hair in what we called "banana curls." I wore my prettiest dress, knowing he would take me around to his colleagues and show off his "beautiful little sweetheart." Obviously, at an early age I knew a lot about seduction. Tell me, what little boy that age would do the same thing?

Fantasy Lovers and Macho Men

Growing up, you and I worked hard at being as beautiful, as provocative, as Marilyn Monroe, Sophia Loren, and Kim Novak. Reel life influenced us enormously. Do you remember sitting breathlessly in the movie theater waiting for Elizabeth Taylor or Audrey Hepburn to get her first kiss? The magic of such moments, the gestures, the glances, the fraught-with-meaning hesitations had a profound effect on us. Of course, we couldn't wait to put what we saw into practice. You knew the effect of accidentally brushing hands when you and that handsome teenaged boy were in the library, presumably doing a homework assignment together. You knew what it was like to catch a stranger's eye across a crowded room. This kind of planning and yearning and dreaming about fantasy lovers gives women an advantage when it comes to attracting a real live man.

Men, on the other hand, have grown up learning that they mustn't cry, mustn't show their feelings except for those of anger and aggression. They learn to shun things that are feminine and "sissy." Boys are expected to become "men," so they are taught to avoid "soft" feelings. Unlike girls, they never share their fantasies with a friend. I suspect that, even today, more boys are ashamed of their fantasies than are ashamed of masturbating.

Men are forced to choose careers early in life and then singlemindedly pursue them. Their mission on earth is to better themselves, to get ahead. They are supposed to take disappointment and rejection in stride—and to bounce right back without showing emotion. They are always climbing Mount Everest. Struggle, win, get ahead, don't be soft. That's a big burden to put on anyone, yet it has fallen on most of the males you're ever likely to meet.

No wonder men learn to hide what they are feeling. Of course they get ulcers. They've got longings buried so deeply in them it may seem impossible to dig them out. Society raises men as emotional clods, and then we wonder why they seem that way.

How fortunate for all of us that the roles of men and women are changing. Fewer and fewer members of the new generation are following the pattern of their mothers and fathers, which portends great things for the future. But in the meantime, right now, the men you and I live with and work with and love are likely to see themselves as modern "cave men." They're still fighting saber-toothed tigers.

They tend to think sex, not sensuality. It is all part of the process of "becoming a man:" having a woman, making money, achieving status, defeating enemies, having sex as often as possible, and procreating. Marriage is not a relationship that needs working at—at least not in emotional terms.

I've· talked to many men about this, from the

famous Hugh Hefner to our not-so-famous handyman. The one thing they all have in common is their image of themselves as that of the hunter, the breadwinner, the one *responsible*.

Woman's Work

A dear male friend of mine is married to a beautiful woman who is a top copywriter at an advertising agency. She is a bright, articulate career woman whose name recently appeared in the business section of *The New York Times*. Yet her husband still refers to her career as her "hobby." In this case, because he makes four times the salary she does, you can perhaps understand a little why he would feel that way. But men who earn less than their wives continue to feel they are the "real" breadwinners of the family.

Not too long ago I needed some carpentry work done around the house, and the name of a retired gentleman in the neighborhood was recommended. Since he had to come to the house several times, we got into the habit of having little chats. I discovered that he only works on small jobs that interest him; he really is retired and wants to take it easy. His wife, however, works full-time as a bookkeeper.

I asked him who did the chores around their house, who cooked dinner, who did the marketing. The answer? His wife of course. His attitude was that she is working only because she wants to, not because they need the money—which means it was up to her to fit in the household work around her (you guessed it) "hobby"!

I mention these two men not as examples of male chauvinism (which of course they are), but simply to remind you that the "cave man" attitude in men is quite entrenched. And this is going to color the way a man responds sexually, even if he doesn't go so far as to rip off your clothes and drag you into the bedroom by your hair.

A Reservoir of Feelings

Say the word "sensuality" to a woman, and she conjures up a vision of charged-with-electricity looks between her and a handsome stranger at the other end of the dinner party table. "Sensuality" means revealing gowns and flickering candlelight and exotic perfume.

The same word put before a red-blooded heterosexual male is likely to evoke a picture of a woman completely naked, making love to him. In fact, usually he pictures four or five women simultaneously doing various erotic things to him. In other words, women think of sensuality as a prelude and an ambiance. Men think of it as the main attraction, the sex act itself. It's the entree, not the appetizer. To most men, sensuality means sex. And sex is rather basic and not surrounded with fantasy and flowers the way it is for a lot of women.

Or so we've been told.

The problem with myths is that they all contain a

bit of truth. What I've been saying is true—most men do hide their tender affections, and they are more primitive than we are in their sexual attitudes. But lurking beneath the surface of the average male is a whole reservoir of romantic, sensual feelings waiting to be tapped.

Who Buys Black Lace Nightgowns?

Actually, down deep we've always known that men are tender and even sentimental. We all know how easily hurt they can be. I learned that lesson a long time ago. I remember clearly the summer I was 14 and working as a junior counselor at camp. A boy named Steve, also about 14 or 15, was a "boyfriend" of mine, meaning he walked me back to girls' camp after swimming and we sat together in chapel on Sunday mornings. This had gone on for about two weeks when, one evening, another young man invited me for ice cream after supper hour and I accepted. Steve heard about it. The next day at swimming, Steve and I were having a long serious talk, the kind young teenagers have. Being eternally curious about these strange creatures called boys, I asked him at one point whether he had ever cried. He admitted he had. I asked him when was the last time he cried? "Last night," he said. I deeply regretted my unwitting cruelty—and, I hope, learned something from the experience.

Men themselves are the first to admit they have great sensuality. Of course, what they mean by that may not be what women mean. But it's there, nevertheless. In fact, most men I've talked to recently have used the word *romantic* to describe themselves. "Look," one man said, "it's men who jam the store counters buying things for Valentine's Day and Mother's Day." Another man, when asked about sensuality, told me, "We're always doing things to encourage our wives to be more sexy. Who buys them black lace nightgowns and perfume? Whose idea is it to go to fancy little hideaway restaurants for dinner?" Even Hugh Hefner, a man who has the reputation of being a callous playboy, told me, "At heart, I'm a romantic." And when he described his feelings about the heroes and heroines of olden days, I believed him.

My Wife, Not My Marriage

All right, we agree men have great potential. Here we are, full of our female intuition and sensitivity, ready to unlock a man's inner sensuality if we could just find the key. Of course, it isn't just one key. We're going to use all kinds of devices to turn that lock. But the first step is to undermine some of his more damaging preconceptions.

One of the big problems in making your man a Honeymooner for Life is that he takes marriage for granted. Rarely does a man refer to "my marriage," as a woman will. He talks about "my wife," not "my marriage." He thinks of marriage in concrete terms, not as some amorphous thing existing in the realm of emotions. And if he takes marriage for granted, the chances are he takes you for granted.

"He doesn't even see me any more," a friend confided. What a common complaint this is! Another friend, Nancy, told me, "It doesn't make any difference whether I'm in my scruffy old bathrobe wearing hair curlers or whether I'm all decked out for a party and have just spent $25 on a new hairdo. I'm just good old Nancy to Charlie." Personally, I don't buy this. I think Nancy and Charlie still look at each other, but they end up seeing the same people they've always seen because each acts in the expected way. What they suffer from is very common and very catching, something like a cold. It's what Arnold Bennett called *dailiness*.

At Ease With the Familiar

When a woman and a man first start learning about each other, everything the other person says or does is unexpected. As my friend Gail told me, "The beginning of an affair is always terribly exciting. A new man is like a new Christmas present. Those early times are spent unwrapping and pulling away the tissue paper to see what's inside—and will I like it."

Gail happens to be the kind of person who doesn't want to progress to the next stage. When she gets tired of the affair she's in, she looks for a new one. Never marriage. Maybe she doesn't want the responsibility.

Maybe she likes the excitement of a new beginning. Only her psychiatrist (and maybe her hairdresser) knows for sure.

But what about the legion of us who have chosen marriage? We also know what happens after the beginning: we find ourselves in the middle of the familiar. Which isn't all bad; this is where most of us are comfortable. We are at ease with the familiar. We say we hate boring routine, but it does make life easier. The terrain ahead is not unknown; we're not likely to encounter strange pitfalls and danger along the way. The alarm goes off at the same time every day. The hours for work, for meals, for errands, for TV are the same as the week before. We see the same friends and go to the same kinds of places for vacation. We tend to go back to the same restaurants we've enjoyed before.

Not surprisingly, sensuality does not survive long in the desert of dailiness. Being an orchid, not a cactus, it needs the right growing conditions. It thrives on newness and change. It is cultivated best in an atmosphere of the unexpected, and its medium is the unpredictable.

A Room At the Plaza

Which brings us to a basic maneuver in unlocking both your sensuality and his. I call it the Surprise Technique. It is potent, extremely useful, and easy to put in practice.

Basically, the Surprise Technique is very simple.

You do something different. You break away from the familiar and become a little unpredictable. Change your routine a bit; vary your hours. Instead of always making love after the 11:00 P.M. news on Friday night, try waking him up with some erotic fondling on Friday morning. A sensuous lovemaking session in the early dawn hours can be a wonderful way to start the day.

The easiest way to get out of a "bedroom rut" is to get out of your bedroom. Recently, my friend Lois confided that just in the last month she and her husband Jack have become "lovers" again. And all she did was show imagination on one occasion.

The occasion was Jack's birthday. Lois decided not to buy the usual shirt and tie for him this year. She wanted to do something different. On the morning of his birthday, she called Jack at his office and told him to come to Room 302 in the Plaza Hotel at 6:00 that evening.

When he arrived, he found a note pinned to the door telling him to enter, lock the door behind him, and make himself comfortable on the sofa. Inside, the ceiling was covered with balloons, and on the cocktail table a bottle of champagne sat chilling in an ice bucket. Lois then made her grand entrance from the bathroom, carrying two glasses and singing Happy Birthday.

She was dressed—in high heels and ribbons of every imaginable color. She had tied bows around her neck, streamers around her thighs, silk cords around her ankles.

She announced that every time they took a sip of champagne, they would each untie one ribbon. By the end of the bottle, Jack was tearing away at her ribbons like a child on Christmas morning, and they had a delightful giddy romp all over that room in the Plaza Hotel—on the sofa, on the rug, sitting on the dresser, even between the sheets on the bed. Afterward, they showered together, dressed, and went down for a long romantic birthday dinner at the Oak Room.

Since that evening, which sparked and stimulated both their sexual appetites, they have made love in a motel two blocks from their house, on Jack's desk in his office (during lunch with the door locked), in the back seat of their car, and in their neighbor's swimming pool at 2:00 in the morning. Last week they took an overnight train ride down to Virginia, partly because they could cuddle and couple in their own compartment!

Unpredictability

I'm not suggesting that you make scouting out new terrain your life's work. Just a touch of spice here and there will add piquancy. It's the little "surprises" that make a difference.

For instance, let's take what you wear to bed. I know how easy it is to fall into the habit of having three warm nightgowns for winter and four sets of cotton pajamas for summer, and that's that. But where's the surprise? If you were just beginning an affair with a hot Italian lover, how long would it last if he kept seeing you in the same gown night after night? How then do you expect to keep your husband's interest piqued? All right. Start by paying a visit to the lingerie department—but this time, try to see the display through *his* eyes. For once, pass up the little Lantz number for that filmy black model with the plunging neckline. He's not that type? Well, he's *some* type, so find it. Maybe he goes for the Snow Princess look—you in the middle of mountains of white lace begging to be ravished. Or try a Baby Doll shortie nightie. (That's so popular with men that a money-losing nightclub in Los Angeles has just turned its fortunes around by putting its waitresses into shorties!) You might forget about nighties altogether and try a black push-up bra and bikini panties. Believe me, lots of men love that look.

I discovered this for myself the other day. Bill and I were looking through our mail at breakfast time, and I was flipping through a department store catalog. I pointed to a pretty nightgown on the lingerie page and asked Bill, "How do you like that one?" He pointed to the opposite page, showing a model cavorting in a lacy plunging bra and panties, and said, "I like that one better."

Mind you, I'm not talking about an every-night diet. The idea is to surprise him once in a while. Wear what you usually wear five nights in a row and on the sixth night show up in something different. And, of course, choose something different that will make *you* feel sexy and beautiful too. After all, you know your good features as well as your flaws, so put your best points on display. If you have beautiful breasts and terrible legs, by all means choose something very low-cut but also long and flowing.

If you're going to be horribly embarrassed or self-conscious, you're not going to enjoy yourself—and that's fully as important as your husband enjoying himself. You have to feel sexy before you can act sexy. You have to turn yourself on before you can turn him on.

In the beginnning, however, be open-minded about what you're willing to try. Anything new is always a bit hard to adjust to at first. If you don't let old prejudices inhibit you, you'll not only enjoy yourself more, you'll find that you're in touch with your sensual feelings in a way you may not have been before.

I know one woman who thought herself too shy to engage in such "silly behavior" as dressing up in different costumes for her husband. But after she did it once or twice—with results that surprised even her— she got into the swing of it. Today, she has escalated her dressing-for-different-roles campaign into a Cecil B. DeMille production. Her closets are full of outfits that turn her into an exotic belly dancer, a topless go-go girl, a gypsy, a willing slave. Her dresser drawers overflow with G-strings, crotchless panties, cut-out bras, and she has the most complete collection I've ever seen of sexy high-heeled shoes. Does her husband watch television every night until he rolls over and goes to sleep? You bet he doesn't!

The Wrong Result

The Surprise Technique works best when employed judiciously. You have to know your man and, obviously, use your awareness of what he is likely to consider a pleasant surprise and vice versa. Don't make the mistake of misjudging the gentleman's reactions. One woman who wanted to introduce her husband to some variations in oral sex decided to try a practice sometimes known as *yalamac*, in which one partner pours liquor or brandy on the genitals of the other and then licks it off. Unfortunately, this didn't appeal to her man at all. He didn't like the feel of the cold liquor on his skin, he was distracted by the smell, and he hated the wet sheets.

You win some, and lose some, but even when your idea doesn't work out exactly as you hoped, your man is going to love the attention he's getting and love you for making the effort.

A serious blunder was committed by one woman who, having read a book on male sexual fantasies, arranged for the services of a female prostitute in order to have a *ménage à trois* at home one night. Her husband was profoundly upset at what he considered immoral and irrational behavior. As a result, he insisted she see a psychiatrist and for months he avoided sexual relations with her.

The moral is: don't let the Surprise Technique become a Shock Technique. Use it the way you would red pepper. A little can go a long way.

Learning To Like Him

Judy and I were classmates at Hunter College in New York. When she married, I have to admit I felt sorry for her. Judy, a graduate of a college noted for its "brainy" women, is a tall slim brunette, quite attractive, a legal secretary who earns a very good living. Ted worked with his father who owned a not-very-successful printing business. Ted was neither ambitious, nor smart, nor good-looking. What did she see in him?

While preparing this book, I taped a long afternoon's talk with Judy. This is her story.

"I knew what everyone thought when I said I was going to marry Ted. My family was appalled. My father did everything short of lock me into my room. At my family's insistence, I even went to a family friend, a therapist who gave me a pretty convincing lecture about women who are sexually attracted to men they know in their hearts aren't good for them. The essence of his lecture was that some women have a low opinion of themselves and seek out marriage partners who, on the face of it, are going to prove disappointing. He said there's a touch of sado-masochism in such relationships, because women like that are not attracted to men who are worthy of them—a phrase I particularly hate.

"This analysis certainly didn't apply to me. I didn't consider myself unworthy, unattractive, inferior, or anything of the kind. What the therapist didn't take into consideration was the fact that I intended to change Ted. The first day it occurred to me that I might marry him, I remember thinking of the ways in which I would change him.

"About a month after the wedding I was feeling terribly depressed. I wasn't actually sorry I had gotten married, but I wondered why I was so depressed and whether that was normal.

"Finally, I went back to see the therapist. This time, he wasn't interested in telling me about women who married men unsuitable for them. He discussed the unrealistic expectations many women have about marriage, how they seem to feel that because they've found a husband, life is suddenly going to be completely different and ecstatic.

"He explained that this kind of euphoria can't last because it is based on a false view of life. Life isn't just a steadily climbing golden road to the final goal of paradise. When that realization overtakes a woman, her euphoria goes out the window and depression follows. There's even a feeling that somehow the dream *was* right, and if she hadn't eaten that apple, she'd still be living in the Garden of Eden."

Judy's therapist advised her to think back to the first time she met Ted. What did she find most attractive about him? Judy decided it was his sunny disposition. Ted accepted whatever came his way without grumbling, the hard knocks along with the good times. Then there was his loyalty and devotion to his family. He was the youngest child, with three older brothers and an older sister, but he was the one who kept his invalid father's printing business going.

And, more important than anything else, he loved her. All her life Judy had needed love, for she had gotten little at home. Her father and mother were the successful owners of an animal hospital.

"They always spent more time with the animals than they did with me," Judy said. "It was not only their livelihood and a good one, but work they loved. I understood that and sympathized, but deep down I never accepted it. I wanted my parents to love *me*. My brother and I were close for a time until he got interested in his studies—he wanted to be a doctor—and in girls. So when Ted came around I was ready to be grateful for the kind of uncritical admiration he offered."

Ted earned less than Judy did, and although they had their own living expenses to contend with, he continued to work at his family's profitless printing shop. There was no future in it; sooner or later the business was bound to go under.

There were other problems too, but the therapist helped Judy to decide that if she wasn't happy with Ted, the fault was hers. *He* hadn't changed. It was she who had not been willing to take him on his own terms. She had contributed a good deal to the current trouble in her marriage by ignoring Ted's virtues and concentrating on his faults. In a real sense, she had not married Ted; she had married the man she intended to change him into.

I'll return to Judy later, but I cite her experience here as an example of a delusion shared by too many women. They can't accept that marriage is a union of two flesh-and-blood human beings, with all their faults and virtues inextricably mingled. They still believe that marriages are made in heaven, not on earth.

Who Is This Stranger I Married?

When Lorraine and Bob were married in 1969, they had known each other a large part of their lives. They had been dating since their last year in school.

"We certainly had no reason to expect any surprises when we were married," Lorraine told me. "I couldn't have thought of any secrets I had from Bob if I tried. I was quite sure we knew everything there was to know about each other.

"Was I wrong! Being married is a lot different than dating. It's better and worse, but mostly different. There were times during that first year—the first few months especially—when I thought that we had gotten all mixed up at the wedding ceremony and I'd married a complete stranger."

I interviewed Bob separately and he was candid about his feelings. "After we were married, I recall thinking that Lorraine certainly must have gone to a lot of trouble to cover up her eccentric habits. Here's one example. We had managed to get away for a few weekends together before we were married, and she always slept in the nude, like I did. On our honeymoon, she wore shortie nightgowns or a slinky black negligee. Then, on our first night in our new home, she showed up for bed wearing flannel pajamas. I couldn't believe it. She told me that from November to April she always wore flannel pajamas because she got cold at night.

"The next few months there seemed to be one little surprise after the other. She couldn't get up in the morning to make my breakfast; in fact she could hardly be spoken to until after her first cup of coffee. Somehow, when we spent a weekend together, she'd managed to be alert and lively. She said that was because it was all so romantic and exciting."

"I admit there are certain things about my habits that I didn't actually publicize before we were married," Lorraine says. "But Bob had some surprises in store for me too. He likes to read at night and keeps the lights on when I want to go to sleep. He smokes too much, and always puts out his cigarettes on his dinner plate. And he's also a compulsive user of 'easy credit' cards. He spends money freely on everything from golf and tennis balls to taxis and phonograph records. As a result, there's often not enough money at the end of the month to pay dentist bills or car insurance, not to mention putting money away to buy the new sofa we need in the living room."

"I think our real selves were in hibernation until we got married," Bob concludes. "The funny part is we never even thought about these things all the years we knew each other. Probably we were glamorizing our images a little. If someone had told us these things, we would have dismissed them as unimportant. But in marriage, they can loom pretty big. In fact, they can begin to drive you crazy."

Differences can lead to an estrangement or they can provide a stimulus for growth rather than a threat. When disagreement exists between a wife and husband, both are prodded into examining their deeper feelings. This can lead to a better level of understanding.

Fortunately, Lorraine and Bob were realistic enough to accept each other's faults and concentrate on enjoying each other's good qualities. Both were willing to work to improve their marriage and compromise their differences, because they basically liked each other—warts and all, as the saying goes.

Crossing a Mine Field

Not all couples are so fortunate. For many, once the minister, priest, or rabbi says they are man and wife, it means they can relax and let more of their real selves hang out. This not only includes some definite, identifiable habits such as those Lorraine and Bob mentioned, but far less identifiable aspects of personality. No matter how open they were with each other before marriage, there has been some pretending. Now, the marriage license gives them license to stop pretending.

This can be startling to the newly married. Adjusting to each other's foibles takes effort. Two people never know all there is to know about each other. What a newly married couple previously knew about each other is only the top of the ant heap. Underneath, there are all sorts of byways and channels through which unseen creatures are scurrying.

This transition period of marriage is comparatively neglected by researchers and by those who deal with marriage in books or portray it on film. Yet it is precisely during this period that most problems arise. The first months, or even years, of marriage are a little like crossing a minefield—in which any moment something may trigger an explosion that will blow you skyhigh.

Often it is the little things that ruin sensual feeling in a marriage: a husband's snoring or repeating the same phrases over and over or laughing too loud at his own jokes. But it's important to distinguish between a partner's quirks and foibles, and the emotional direction in which a marriage is traveling.

You can easily deal with little annoying habits. Get yourself earplugs so that his snoring won't bother you, tune out when he keeps using the same phrases. And the next time you both hear a comedian on TV, casually point out how rarely a professional comic ever laughs at his own jokes. These little pushes and pulls, adjustments and accommodations, are of no more consequence than the tiny shifts of direction of the steering wheel when you're driving a car. What really matters is where the car is going.

When a wife complains to me about her husband's quirks and foibles, I tell her to check on her own. Do you never stop talking, or never listen? Do you interrupt when he's speaking? Pry through his papers? Do you monopolize the telephone? Are you *always* late getting ready while he has to sit around waiting to leave the house? Nobody is perfect. Just ask an eraser.

His and Hers

"I never realized there were going to be such difficulties in adjusting to Hank," says Bernice. "I knew we'd have some problems—practical and emotional—to overcome, but not as big as they turned out to be. To begin with, we had differing interests. For some reason, this didn't strike me as a big problem when we were dating. But Hank's an outdoor type who loves camping trips, horseback riding, long hikes, and mountain climbing, and he's an amateur botanist. I'm interested in dancing, sketching, needlework, and cooking.

"I love to cook gourmet meals, for example. But

Hank is a vegetarian who won't touch meat, poultry, or fish. All he wants are vegetables, fruit, cheese, eggs, and nuts. When we were dating he always took me to glamorous eating places where we had wine and danced, and I never paid much attention to the fact that he was ordering unglamorous meals. I wouldn't have thought it was a problem anyway, but when meal after meal is always the same I go a little cook-happy. It's no fun, not to mention damned uneconomical, to make gourmet meals for one. Even when I made dinner for friends, there he'd sit with his fruit and cheese and nuts.

"Another major surprise was relatives. Before we were married, even during our engagement, which lasted almost two years, we got along fine with our relatives. But after we were married, those relatives suddenly became in-laws. We were *involved* with them. I found it very uncomfortable. I particularly found Hank's parents hard to get along with. Finally, to avoid confrontations or quarrels, Hank put another phone into our apartment with a different number. Only his parents had the number and he was the only one who answered it, so I never had to talk to them. They never knew about the separate phone—we told them our number had been changed—and that made the situation easier to accept."

This small change had a big effect on Bernice. After a while she discovered that she wasn't as angry at Hank's parents as she had been. "I can put up with an occasional dinner with them. I just couldn't take the constant harassment on the telephone," is the way she put it.

A marriage is continually being shaped out of the sum of a couple's experiences together. It is important never to let any disagreement become so charged with hostile emotion that it begins to affect how much you love each other. Keep trying to find ways to split the difference, and time works on your side. Within any good marriage, there is a slow, almost imperceptible drift toward each other. A wife and husband who honestly try to satisfy each other's needs will benefit from the delicate on-going process of mutual accommodation. Disharmony lessens with time, and a conflict that was once in sharp focus becomes blurred and indistinct.

We all know the old saying that familiarity breeds contempt. But it isn't true that long-term intimacy inevitably leads to that kind of feeling. Not at all. Time itself can never destroy real intimacy. True intimacy is a creation *of* time. Whatever attracted you to each other in the first place is more likely to increase as you share your lives and your deepest emotions, as you come to depend on the affection and support and understanding of someone. That kind of familiarity breeds neither contempt nor indifference—but love.

Adjustments and Advantages

When previous patterns of behavior are disrupted, that also causes marital conflict.

"I used to go bowling after work with a few friends," Wayne told me. "We'd have a couple of beers, and place some small bets among ourselves.

When I got married the owner of the place told me, 'Well, I won't be seeing much of you any more.' I thought he was kidding. But, sure enough, Meg wanted me home after work. She didn't like to hold dinner till late, or eat it alone. That annoyed me. I still had an image of myself as being free to go where I liked and do what I wanted. But now I had to make allowances for her likes and wants. We more or less straightened it out. I still do go bowling—only every other week—and somehow it isn't as much fun as it used to be."

These are the sort of situations unforeseen by couples who are entering marriage. The need to make adjustments can make for friction.

On the other hand, there are compensating advantages. Once the initial adjustments have been worked out—and this requires an ability on both sides to rock the boat without swamping it—there are many ways in which the sensual content of a marriage can be enriched. These methods can be small in themselves, but their cumulative impact is large because they are renewable every day of your married life.

The two of you aren't likely to have forgotten the secret glow you felt the first time you introduced your partner as "my husband" or "my wife." Well, there's no reason for that glow to fade if you don't let perfunctoriness take over. You are saying something important each time you say, "I'd like you to meet my husband (or wife)." You are saying, "This is the one person in the world I have chosen to live with." "Wife" and "husband" are in a sense inadequate terms—

inadequate to express all that is contained in them. If you are aware of that each time you make such an introduction, your voice will have that special lilt in it— implying "and isn't he (she) wonderful!" A small verbal caress can do more than you think. Try it.

It also helps to have an endearing private nick-name. If a man often calls his wife "Beautiful," he is giving her a tiny sign of his love. If this becomes a habit, he will condition himself to think of her that way, and she will become more beautiful—for him.

"Guess Who?"

Flirting can give a sure-fire stimulus to any marriage. I mean, of course, flirting with each other. Married people are so often burdened down with problems, finances, children—the problems and routines of the day or week—that they become working partners rather than loving partners. They tend to forget what attracted them to each other in the first place.

Recently, celebrating the silver wedding anniversary of our friends Edith and Julian, I couldn't help noticing Edith playing up to her husband of 25 years as if she were a young single woman intent on making a conquest. I saw the way she looked at Julian over the rim of her champagne glass, and when someone offered a toast to the "youngest married lovers we know," Edith whispered "amen" to Julian and linked her arm in his. I also noticed that she slipped him a note under her napkin just as dinner was ending.

I asked her what was in the note, explaining that I was writing a book on the subject of marriages that had become honeymoons for life.

The note, in its entirety: *I can't wait to be alone with you. Guess who?*

Not surprisingly, Julian also played the role of an amorous gallant. At one point, as Edith was going off to freshen her makeup, she said, "Excuse me. I have to make myself gorgeous." Julian instantly replied, "You don't have to do a thing," and the sincerity with which he said it sent rumblings of jealousy all up and down the line of all the women within hearing distance. That, I remember thinking, is one marriage no one has to worry about.

A Hum in the Mind

Remember my friend Judy, whose problems I described at the beginning of this chapter? When she faced the fact that all her efforts had created nothing but unhappiness for her and for Ted, Judy had to ask herself the question: Do I really want this marriage to be saved? Or do I want to leave Ted and find somebody more suitable?

She decided that Ted was the man she wanted. "If you can't leave the man, love him." This shift in attitude brought about a dramatic change. Ted, who had begun to feel frustrated, baffled, and finally resentful, became a more confident and capable husband.

And the two of them became much happier as a married couple.

I asked Judy to summarize her part in this "miracle." Here's what she came up with:

- Never nag. If you feel strongly that something ought to be changed, say so. Say it once—then forget it.
- Never treat your husband as anything less than your equal. He is a separate person, not a part of you nor an object to be manipulated by you.
- Accept your husband as the man he is—with all his faults and virtues. Then concentrate as little as possible on those faults he's unwilling or unable to change—and use that leftover energy in concentrating on his virtues.
- Never let sensuality go out of your marriage.

That last point deserves being set down in capital letters: NEVER LET SENSUALITY GO OUT OF YOUR MARRIAGE.

A marriage without sensuality is a working arrangement, a room-and-board accommodation, or a friendship—it is definitely *not* a marriage. And I'd like to emphasize, again, that I'm not just talking about sex. Sex is marvelous, it is the peak of sensuality, but it is, after all, relatively infrequent. What about the other 23½ hours in the day?

Between a wife and husband there can be either a shallow sexual relationship or one based on mutual acceptance and appreciation. Most marital relationships begin on a shallow level through sexual stimulation ("He wants me; I want him") and too many end there. Other couples grow into a deeper sense of commitment and mutual discovery. And this is what gives them the opportunity to keep on developing.

Remember that sensuality does not have to be fierce or demanding; it can be an activity that sets up a kind of pleasant hum in the mind. If you speak to someone with a special note of affection in your voice, you are being sensual. A lingering kiss on the cheek, or a quick hug, or setting out his morning paper turned to the page he likes to read first can be sensual. If you serve him a favorite Sunday breakfast treat on a Wednesday morning, or save for him a magazine article you know he'd enjoy and may have missed, or touch feet with him in bed just before going off to sleep, you are being sensual.

Wrong Number? Keep Trying

Men like this kind of sensuality almost as much as a direct sexual overture. To a man, unlike most women, the sex act represents a challenge. Fear of impotence is strong in most men, as sex surveys attest, so he is likely to approach each encounter something like Bruce Jenner coming up for the next event in the decathlon. The sex act involves questions of his masculinity, his achievement, his youth and virility, even his own picture of himself as a member of a dominant, rather than submissive, species.

With all the doubts and complexities surrounding

the sex act for men, we might reasonably wonder why they enjoy sex as much as they do. Certainly they deserve understanding and sympathy—along with a little space in which to strut and fret. We can even create an environment in which they can thrive.

This does not mean, however, that we have to treat them as a rare species of hothouse plant. If you have a day when your husband is simply too irritating for you to bear without speaking up, then do. Get it off your bosom. Put it out of your mind.

That night, or the next day, try again to be a loving, sensual wife. Keep trying, even if he's still being difficult. Try, try again to get through. Sooner or later, you're likely to communicate. When Alexander Graham Bell invented the telephone, the first call he made was probably to a wrong number.

Find the Right String and Pull It

This approach to marriage has worked for millions. It certainly worked for Maria and Craig, who were beginning to drift apart. The signs were painfully clear: sooner or later in any conversation, whether in a large or small group, they began to snipe at each other. One afternoon, during a visit to our home, Maria confided in me that Craig had lost interest in having sex with her.

"Right after dinner each night," Maria told me, "he plunks himself down in front of television. I do the dishes and evening chores, and by the time I finish he's in bed. When I come in, he's either asleep or pretending to be asleep. A few times I've tried to kiss him or touch him, but I never get any response. Just a sleepy grunt before he turns over on his side. I'm not going to force the issue. If he wants sex, he's going to have to take the initiative."

I was in the middle of research for this book, and I told Maria what I had discovered from people whose marriages were in many ways like an extended honeymoon. She shook her head, unbelieving. It sounded too simple for Maria. It wouldn't work. "My marriage is over," she announced dramatically.

I persuaded her to give the Sensual Solution a try. "I grant you, it does sound very simple. But if you add just one new way of behaving—even the simplest—you might change the whole situation. Every marriage is a tangled heap of everything, good or bad, great or terrible. Find the right string and pull it, and the whole tangled heap may unwind for you."

Maria was not convinced, but she said she'd give it a try. The next time I spoke to her, she was excited. "It's all so different. Craig is kind and considerate and generous. And we're so much happier now. I really don't understand why it works like this—but it certainly does. Thanks so much!"

What was the Sensual Solution? Nothing very earthshaking—just some guidelines that helped Maria keep romance alive in her marriage:

- Communicate. A sensual thought is wasted when it's not communicated. Sensuality should be open and honest. If you're having breakfast and you find yourself dwelling fondly on how you made love last night, say so. *Communicate.* That's the first and indispensable step toward lovemaking, isn't it? Let him know that the feel of his body against yours is one of the chief reasons you think life is wonderful. Don't just tell him in words—show him. If he happens to come nude out of the shower, whistle at him. Or better, ask if you can touch. Or still better, touch without asking. If he makes an advance, respond. If he keeps on making advances, don't retreat. Surrender.

• In lovemaking, change your approach frequently. Make love at different times, under different circumstances, in different places, in different ways. Spur-of-the-moment lovemaking can be delicious. It really won't ruin your day if dinner is half an hour late or you don't arrive exactly on the minute for the bridge game at your neighbor's house.

• When you're feeling tired, overworked, or exhausted, don't try to force yourself to be sensual. There are times when even the lustiest of lovers would rather use a bed just to sleep in. If at all possible, go away together—even if only overnight. Then don't waste a minute. Arrange your schedule so you have all the time and leisure you need for making love.

Alive Among the Dead

A man needs loving sympathy and sensual comfort when he's not coping well in other areas of his life. My friend Miriam, who now has a spectacularly successful marriage, told me of the serious problem she had during the eighth year with her husband Ken.

"I was earning good money as an assistant sales manager in a department store, and Ken was working only part time. He was a compulsive student, who already had a couple of college degrees—one in science, another in education—and was going on for his Ph.D. in education. He had to study very hard and hold a part-time job, so his schedule was impossible. And I not only had to handle a full-time job, but do the cooking, cleaning, and even haul out the garbage.

"Whenever he had a spare few hours, Ken spent them with his teenaged brother who was a nut on geology. They would go off on rock hunting expeditions while I stayed home to clean house. I thought it was unfair. I made my attitude clear to Ken, even when I didn't put it in words. When I wasn't actually picking on him, I was sending out hostile vibes. I remember telling my mother at the time, 'If I didn't keep after him every minute, he'd never stir himself to do anything. All he does is bury his nose in a book!'"

Miriam's feeling that Ken was an unsatisfactory husband brought them close to a divorce. One day Miriam asked herself, What's gone wrong? She recalled their first years as being heavenly, even though the situation had been much the same. They had lived in a tiny efficiency apartment, Ken was studying for his bachelor's degree in education, and Miriam paid all the bills and did all the housework. Yet she recalled that period as the best of her marriage.

As she put it: "I used to walk the street on my way to work, seeing all the tired, harassed, nervous people going by. And I'd think to myself that to be in love, as I was, was like being alive among so many dead.

"Well, now I was one of the tired, nervous, harassed people. The outward circumstances of my life hadn't changed. So the change had to be in me. I had stopped tolerating the things I'd tolerated so easily before. I wasn't able to love Ken, not fully. And the inevitable result was that he didn't love me either."

Miriam made up her mind then and there to stop blaming Ken for what wasn't his fault and to be more supportive and understanding. Ken had always had potential, and they had always cared for each other. He was a worthwhile person, deserving of love, and she had been withholding it, giving him little but criticism. Her main role in life had become that of chief nag, one she wasn't at all happy playing.

"From that moment, I changed for the better. And Ken came alive, began helping me around the house and spending weekends with me instead of with his brother. A few months later, Ken got his doctorate, and a very desirable job offer.

"What worked these changes? Just my attitude. What Ken needed was a heavy dosage of what I call the three A's—acceptance, approval, admiration. It sounds so amazingly simple I can hardly believe it myself. But that's the god's truth."

Because Miriam couldn't accept Ken, she had been slowly turning him into a self-doubter, someone who might have become a failure. Today, Miriam and Ken are happy with each other and their home is overflowing with warmth and love. I didn't have to ask her what the sensual quotient of her marriage was. It was evident in every gesture, every glance that passed between her and Ken.

The Golden Rules

How do you get started on becoming sensual lovers?

It needn't be complicated. You learn to accept, really accept, the man you're living with. You appreciate his good qualities, and you let him know it—by words, actions, and those all-important unspoken vibrations.

Let him know that the main thing you like about him is simply—*him*. A woman may sometimes wonder why her husband stays with her, commutes to work, does the chores around the house, delivers his paycheck to meet the bills. He could hire someone to cook and clean, and he wouldn't have to look far to satisfy his sexual needs either. What's the answer? The answer is *her*.

Now turn that situation on its head for a minute, and you can see why it's important that you let him know why you stay with him. He's wondering whether all you really see in him is a good provider, a hard worker, a companion for going out, a handyman and mechanic, a sexual partner. He needs reassurance as much as you do.

By all means, let him know as often as you can that you value him not for what he does, but for himself. No other provider or companion or handyman could fill the bill. That's the kind of security everyone needs—to be liked, admired, and loved, not for the things about us that can so easily change, but for the one unchangeable and permanent thing: ourselves.

When your husband knows that he is accepted and loved for this reason, you're likely to find yourself with a man who wants to please you as much as you please him.

It's hard to imagine an unhappy marriage in which both partners share the following attitudes and emotions:

1. Liking your partner, as a person.
2. Admiring and respecting your partner.
3. Feeling relaxed and at ease with each other.
4. Accepting the value of qualities that may not be your own.
5. Feeling a sense of security and trust.
6. Considering the other's happiness equal in importance to your own.

7. Enjoying a strong bond of physical intimacy.
8. Being able to confide your deepest-felt emotions and experiences, sharing your triumphs and failures.
9. Having a mutual sense of humor and fun.
10. Allowing each other to be self-reliant—a separate planet, not a satellite.

These are the ten golden rules of sensuality—and as good a prescription as I know for anyone who wants to be a Honeymooner for Life!

Training
To
Be
Sensual

A woman who lets her muscles grow slack, her body become flaccid, sends out negative sensual vibes. The young woman, once proud of her figure, who used to go to exercise class three times a week, now eats too many fattening desserts, has an extra drink when she shouldn't, probably smokes too much—and certainly exercises too little. Soon her figure leaves everything *not* to be desired.

The same is true of men—even more so. That fine young hard-chested, flat-bellied man, who once looked so great in swimming trunks at the beach, somehow is transformed into a slouching, paunchy parody of himself who sits glazed in front of the TV set watching sports he no longer engages in. He gets out of breath running for a bus, and when he has to climb stairs he wheezes with the effort. Because he knows the shape he's in, he feels less sensual, acts less romantic, and makes love less and less frequently.

Many, many couples become unattractive to each other simply because they let their physical equipment rust. It is easy enough to turn out the lights when making love, but it is not so easy to shut out the image of a physically undesirable body. And the tactile sense may also be sending back unsensual messages to the brain.

Regular care and exercise will help anyone maintain an energetic, well-proportioned, sexually attractive body. That body needs to be in condition for you to enjoy a good sex life, because making love is vigorous exercise in itself. A good session in bed is roughly equivalent to running a 60-meter dash. Your heartbeat will increase from as low as 70 beats a minute to almost 200 beats a minute, and is accompanied by a corresponding tripling of your respiration rate. That amounts to an expenditure of physical energy that no athlete would try to make without training. Yet millions of out-of-shape married people do exactly that, week after week. The results aren't good for their health, and their poor performance in the boudoir has a bad effect on their marriage. A really satisfying sex act requires, in addition to the right ambiance and the right emotional attitude, a certain amount of sheer physical stamina. You'd really better be in condition.

The neuromuscular system affects such crucial factors as sexual timing and coordination. Just as no one can pick up a tennis racket and perform like a player who has trained, coordinated muscles and nerves, so no one can be really proficient in sex without some physical training.

As Bonnie Prudden says: "A Beethoven sonata will always sound better on a concert piano than on a kazoo." If you are out of condition for the kind of exercise required in the bedroom, there are easy ways to improve. It's perfectly possible to increase the movement of important joints by making muscles, tendons, and ligaments more flexible and bringing unused muscles into play. You can gain better control over the movements of your body, thereby increasing your skill.

In recent years we have learned a great deal about training muscles to work better without strain. Much of what we've learned is applicable to the nation's favorite indoor sport.

The following exercises will help to increase your body's strength, stamina, flexibility, freedom of movement, muscle tone—and, as a result, perform better. An incidental benefit is that you'll look better and feel better.

Increased trunk flexibility. Stand erect, then bend your body forward, keeping your knees straight. Stand erect again, then bend backward from the waist as far as you can. Each time, try to move your body a little farther forward and backward. On the forward move, try to touch the floor with your hands. On the backward move, try to reach farther and farther with your hands down your legs—to the backs of your knees and below.

Now do an equal number of body-swaying movements. Standing erect once more, arms at your sides, bend to your left, reaching down on your leg as far as you can with your left hand. Then bend to your right, reaching down on your right leg with your right hand. The bending should be performed in a kind of left-to-right swaying movement.

Strength and control in your lower back and thighs. Kneel on the floor, sitting with your buttocks on your heels. Bend forward at the waist as far as you can, letting your arms and hands drag behind until you touch the floor with your face. Return to kneeling position again. Repeat no more than ten times.

Now, while kneeling on the floor, place your hands on your hips and bend back slowly. Straighten up, then try to bend back a little farther. Feel the muscles stretching in your hips, thighs, and back? Return to a kneeling position, and now bend forward until you can place your forearms on the floor in front of you and rest your forehead on them. Keeping your forearms resting on the floor, rock forward and backward as far in each direction as possible.

Conditioning the pelvis. Unhappily, there are few activities in modern life that call for pelvic movement. The thrusting back and forth of the pelvis is limited to the act of sexual intercourse and to the more energetic dance movements. As a result, important muscles in the pelvic area lose strength, suppleness, and the ability to coordinate properly.

The following exercises are designed to restore power and flexibility to your pelvic area, so that you can intensify the forward and backward motion used in making love. An active pelvic thrust during the sex act adds a great deal to the stimulation and satisfaction of your partner. Basically, what you are doing in these exercises is what a burlesque dancer does when executing a "bump."

• Stand against a wall with your feet together and your heels, buttocks, and the back of your head pressed against the wall. Pull in your stomach. Now, thrust your pelvic region (your genital area) forward and upward, while you slide your buttocks down the wall and try to press the small of your back flat against the wall.

  Reverse the action. Hollow the small of your back (pull it away from the wall), and slide your buttocks up against the wall to the highest level you can reach. Try to thrust your buttocks backward and upward, and rotate as if you were indeed doing a "buttocks bump" in a burlesque house.

  Now alternate, going first in one direction, then the other. Strive for the furthest possible range of movement in both the up-forward and back-downward tilting. Do this slowly at first, but eventually speed up the movements. As a variation, do the same exercise with your feet spread apart.
• Lying on your back, with legs together and knees straight, arms alongside your body, palms

resting flat on the floor, perform the identical pelvic thrust. Then do it with your legs spread apart.

- Lie on your back with your knees together, but this time bent so that your feet are flat on the floor. Put your arms above your head, resting the back of hands on the floor. Raise your buttocks completely up from the floor, and then perform the same pelvic thrusts.
- Lie on your left side with legs and body straight. Place your right hand on the floor, in front of your chest, for balance. Do the same back-and-forth pelvic thrusts. Reverse and repeat the exercise while lying on your right side.
- You can practice the pelvic thrust while sitting on a chair. Sit on the edge of the chair, reach behind you and grasp the sides of the chair. Supporting yourself on your arms, do your "bumps."
- Conclude your pelvic exercises with some side-to-side action. Stand erect, hands at your sides. Thrust your hips to the left, then to the right. Your legs and body should remain almost still, while your pelvis moves from side to side. Strive for the utmost possible range of movement. A useful trick is to stand in an open doorway and try to reach out with each hip to touch the sides of the doorjamb. You can't, but try anyway.

These very simple exercises, practiced faithfully, will enable you to get more pleasure from sex because the pelvic thrust exposes your clitoris to maximum stimulation. This thrusting action is the surest route to orgasm. In fact, there is no more important contribution your body can make to the sex act than the pelvic thrust. The more effective it is, the more pleasure you—and your partner—will experience. And if you're one of the too many women who lie passively without contributing any action during lovemaking, this simple technique can change the whole character of the act.

The vaginal contraction. By using her interior muscles, a woman can intensify sexual pleasure for both herself and her man. Vaginal muscles tend to suffer from disuse; about the only time we use these muscles is when we contract them to "hold in" a full bladder. You will need practice before you are able to strengthen your vaginal muscles to the point that you can control them effectively while making love, but if you persevere, the contractions will get stronger.

Lie on your back. Concentrate on those vaginal muscles, and try as hard as you can to contract them. Hold for a count of ten, then relax. Actually, you can perform this exercise at any time of the day or during any other activity—while standing, sitting, lying down, walking, driving a car, even at a cocktail party. No one is going to know what you're doing with your vaginal muscles unless he happens to be making love to you at that moment!

The buttocks muscles. These are important in lovemaking. By tensing and relaxing your buttocks, you add a new experience to sexual encounters.

You probably haven't heard about the importance

of the buttocks muscles during the sex act because so few people control these muscles. Almost anyone can tense and relax the buttocks, but that's about all. If you want to see real control, watch a beginner's class in ballet. The instructor usually tries to lecture the dancers on how to draw in their derrières. He tells them to contract the gluteus maximus muscles. Some get the point and begin doing it right away. Others will be mystified—until the instructor pushes a half-dollar in between their buttocks cheeks. In approximately one second the student finds out exactly what is meant: without any need of further instruction, the gluteus maximus muscles contract to hold the coin in place. The student, with tightened derrière, then goes on to perform the beginning movements of ballet.

The following exercises are intended to give you increased control of the buttocks muscles so rarely used in ordinary activity. Once you've got control of your gluteal muscles, you are ready for the "derrière clamp"—and I guarantee you'll start to enjoy sexual intercourse more.

- Sit on the floor with your legs fully extended and your hands resting lightly, palms down, on your knees. Lean back slightly. Tighten your buttock muscles to help maintain your balance. *Squeeze* the "cheeks" together, and hold them that way for a long count of ten. Relax completely. Repeat five times. Do the same exercise with your legs extended and apart. Repeat five times.

- Lie on your right side, supporting yourself with your left hand on the floor in front of your chest. Do the "gluteal squeeze" five times. Reverse to your left side, and repeat the squeeze five times.
- Lie on your stomach, resting your head on bent elbows. Squeeze your derrière and, at the same time, push your pubic area hard against the floor. (Use a pillow underneath.) Hold tension in both areas for the same slow count of ten.
- Turn over on your back; extend your arms above your head, back of hands flat on the floor. Fully extend your legs and press them tightly together. In this position, practice the derrière clamp. At the same time, squeeze your thighs together and make an attempt to contract your vaginal muscles. Hold for a count of ten.

Alternately contracting and tensing all these internal muscles during lovemaking will help you to reach a more intense and satisfying orgasm. Don't wait until orgasm is underway, or even until shortly before orgasm begins (when you know it is coming)—but start from the moment of penetration. Your husband will find the experience stimulating, too!

Marvelous Control

"When I was single," Sandy said, "I used to take pride in making it with a different girl every week. After I slept with a girl a few times, I more or less lost interest in having sex with her. It all became too boring and predictable. The thing I really wanted was novelty and variety, and I thought the only way to get it was to try sleeping with many different girls. Then I met Yvonne.

"She didn't seem too interested in me, and that caught my interest. She became a challenge. The first time I asked her to go to bed with me, she warned me that she wouldn't 'fake it' or let me off easy.

"I'd never met a woman like her, and I tried to put her in her place by telling her I didn't perform for anybody. But I kept thinking of her going out with other men and it was gnawing at my insides. Finally I called her. I figured I'd show her something—after all, I'd had plenty of experience.

"She's the one who showed me. I'd never had a woman who had such marvelous control of her body. It took me forever to climax. She'd bring me up to it, and then cool me off. I never worked harder in bed—and never had a better time.

"I didn't intend to get married until I was at least 35, but I was frightened of losing Yvonne. I proposed— and she accepted!"

In this true story, I'm sure you didn't overlook the reference to Yvonne's control of her body. The exercises I've outlined in this chapter will help you achieve the same kind of control.

To quote Bonnie Prudden again: "It's important to remember that what you don't use, you lose. That includes your ability to make love. If you've gone off the beam, you can certainly get back on again. All it takes is time and patience. And effort."

Don't do the exercises once or twice, and then forget about them. Do them faithfully and your sex life will move out of the humdrum and into the wow!

Homely Advice

During one of my interviews for this book, I spoke with a woman who assured me that her marriage—already 16 years old—was a very happy one. She and her husband had reached a stage of sexual abstinence, but she didn't consider herself frigid or her husband undersexed. Sex simply wasn't important because, as she put it, "we have everything in common—each other."

Later, I talked to her husband and heard a different version. *He* was not at all happy with the lack of sex in their marriage. "Without physical intimacy, I don't believe you can love a person thoroughly," he told me. He was even having a discreet liaison with another woman. ("I owe it to my wife to keep it a secret from her.") But he wasn't sure how long this arrangement would work.

A woman cannot be a true partner in marriage without actively participating in sex. If she doesn't participate, she's a partner in name only. The psychological problems underlying the marriage I just described are outside the scope of this book—and my competence. But for the wife who simply has trouble feeling in the mood for sex as often as she and her husband would like, I can strongly recommend a simple-to-practice method that has worked for many women.

Never forget: Sensuality is, first, a state of mind, and only second a physical act. This method can be used any time you want to work yourself into the right frame of *mind*.

Suppose your husband is showing signs of warmth and you're feeling like an iceberg. Don't go ahead and make love right then. Your true mood will make you—and your husband—feel that he's taking advantage of you. That doesn't lead to anything but frustration.

Instead, excuse yourself for a few minutes. Let him think you're putting on cologne and a sexy nightgown. In fact, go ahead and do just that. Then find a quiet spot—the bathroom will do just fine—turn off the lights and relax. Close your eyes, let your body go absolutely limp. Think of your feet becoming so soft and nerveless that they're practically falling off your ankles. Now move up to your ankles—think of them as wobbly and loose. Then on to your knees, your thighs, your hips, your stomach, your chest. Let all the muscles go slack and unstrung. Now you have yielded your whole body to this marvelous sense of relaxation. You are disengaged from your surroundings. You aren't really feeling anything.

Keeping yourself in this state of relaxation, become aware of your breathing. Breathe slowly through your nose. You are close to a state of somnolence. As you breathe out, think the words, "Oh, yes," silently. Your breathing should be easy and natural. But continue to repeat your silent "Oh, yes." Continue this for a few minutes—breathing in, out, "Oh, yes."

This method is not unlike transcendental meditation, but there's an important difference: its purpose is not to induce deep relaxation for its own sake. During this sensual meditation, I want your thoughts to wander to the physical delights of sex, the undressing, caressing—whatever sensations you find most exquisite. As you do this, silently chanting, "Oh, yes," you will feel the warmth of desire beginning to invade you. Let it come up through your body. If any thought distracts or disturbs you for a moment, turn your mind blank again. Keep repeating, "Oh, yes," whispering it aloud if that helps. In a few minutes—five to ten at the most—open your eyes. You're ready.

Master this technique, and you'll be able to elicit the Sensual Response whenever you need it.

❦ Turning On

Did you ever hear the advertising slogan: Sell the sizzle, not the steak?

Sex is your steak, sensuality the sizzle. There are only a few grades of steak, but the varieties of sizzle are endless.

If your sex life has become stereotyped or the deadening hand of routine has turned you off, the remedy is at hand.

I'm not talking about 32 new positions for intercourse, or even foreplay. There is plenty of such advice to be found in books and manuals, all too many of which seem designed to take the fun out of fornication. They often leave a woman feeling that she should be a Nadia Comenici in the bedroom, although real sensuality has little to do with gymnastics. What I'm going to be talking about are the simple ways in which a couple can express affection for each other, the fundamentals of sensuality—the ABC's that are too often overlooked by those who try to persuade you to qualify for a Ph.D. in carnal knowledge.

Different strokes for different folks, as the saying goes; what works for a missionary doesn't necessarily work for a cannibal. But a universal need in all the animal kingdoms is for touching. Simple touching, skin against skin, is one of the body's most important needs.

There are many times in a marriage when words either aren't enough, or are too much. You don't speak when you ought to, or you exhaust communication in a lot of talk, talk, talk. What is there left to say?

At such times, you can say a lot by touching. It is a language that preceded words, a language we understood when we were infants, and which on a primal level we still understand better than speech.

Laying On Of Hands

Experiments show that animals learn how to make contact with others of their species by first touching and being touched by their parents. In one experiment, a generation of monkeys was reared with substitute mothers—rag dolls—to which the infant monkeys clung as other monkeys did to their real mothers. Physically, the monkeys in this experiment in deprivation matured normally. But when they were released among other monkeys who had been raised by real mothers, the deprived monkeys were unable to adjust. They did not find mates; they could not perform sexually. Their substitute rag-doll mothers had not taught them, through touching, the invaluable lesson of how to make physical contact.

Human beings are more fortunate in that no one would dare to experiment with them in this way. But human beings are taught to control many of their natural impulses. After the weaning stage, there are areas of the mother's body that a child is not encouraged to touch, nuzzle, or kiss. Before long, she or he is taught to repress other impulses: not to eat with the fingers, not to scream or cry for attention, not to touch dozens—possibly hundreds—of fascinating objects within reach, not to relieve her or himself without going to the bathroom.

These "commandments" get mixed up together. Touching may easily be seen as another impulse not to be indulged if the child is to please her or his parents with her or his progress toward maturity. With the onset of adolescence, she or he may be taught not to practice masturbation. She or he will almost certainly be taught not to have sex on impulse, and she or he will have learned that having sensual feelings for a sibling, or for members of her or his own sex, is terribly wrong.

A male child, once he is past a certain age, is unlikely to be hugged or kissed by his father—or, when he is a little older, by his mother. He learns that touching other males must be confined to a meeting of palms during a handshake. A female child has a better time of it—for a while. She is cuddled by both parents until—suddenly—she's "too big," and that warm hug from Daddy becomes fleeting. This abrupt deprivation may be even worse than the earlier indoctrination the male child gets into the aloof ways of "adult" behavior. Soon the female also learns that a hug or embrace for another female should be brief and discreet. And so the pleasures of touching are restricted and confined.

Yet the need persists, revealing itself in our language. "That was a touching gift," "I was so touched I almost cried," "a touching scene," "a soft touch" (meaning someone who is easily, perhaps too easily, reached by another), "a touchy person" (meaning someone whose feelings are too easily aroused), "a touch of class" (touch has conferred something valuable), or even "touched in the head" (the wrong touch has disturbed the delicate mechanism of the brain).

In more exuberant moments, when circumstances encourage our inhibitions to slip for a moment, we return to touching as a principal means of expressing joy. At an airport, husbands and wives, parents and children, long-parted friends rush into each other's arms. They hold each other tightly, press cheeks together, caress each other's faces, pat each other on their backs, and walk off with arms entwined.

And when television cameras visit the locker room of the World Series winners, notice how often the ballplayers touch each other, clasp each other, ruffle each other's hair, slap behinds, grab each other's arms, and otherwise entangle bodies. In fact, when the last out assures a World Series victory, we see players converging on the pitcher and joining together in what would appear to be a mass orgy of jumping on each other's bodies while trying to embrace.

In any other situation, males acting in such an exuberant fashion would be considered either "touched in the head"—or sexually deviant.

The Art of Seduction

Between a wife and husband, there is much perfunctory touching—the hurried goodbye kiss, the embrace so brief that it can hardly be called an embrace. If touching goes beyond that, however, it is usually understood as an invitation to sexual inter-course. The toucher may be expressing the simple need to make contact, but the kiss or caress is likely to be taken as an invitation as explicit as one put into writing.

In the bedroom, "serious" touching conveys an even clearer message. The contact of body against body if the bodies are wearing nightgowns and pajamas is almost invariably interpreted as, "How about it?" If the bodies happen to be naked at the time, then the question "embodies" its own answer. In bed, wives and husbands deny themselves the pleasure of touch-ing lest their actions be misunderstood. Tired and depressed after a hard day at the office, worried about job or finances, a husband suppresses his need to be comforted. However much he may want the reas-surance of fondling and being fondled, he turns on his side and goes to sleep. A moment that would have significantly enriched a relationship is lost forever.

The right to touch and be touched should be as sacred a part of the marriage contract as sexual fulfillment. A woman who has a baby satisfies her physical need for touching for a time. She bathes and powders, dresses and feeds, holds and carries and kisses the infant. More men are beginning to share these tasks, but the woman usually has much more opportunity. The sheer physical pleasure of snuggling, caressing, rubbing and tickling, sniffing and nibbling, running fingers down the spine or across the belly is a sensual gratification that meets a strong need.

Why should touching between partners in marriage be interpreted as a preliminary to sex? Psychologist Leon Salzman has defined seduction as "any activity that initiates, encourages, or persuades an individual to become involved in intimate relations of some kind." There'd be no quarrel with that definition if "intimate relations" did not mean sexual relations to most people. Unfortunately, it does.

But since we all need touching—the just-plain I-need-comfort kind of touching—don't go through life depriving yourself or your husband. Cuddle up to him and say, "I feel down; I just need to be held." When he's weary or depressed, caress him, hold him, pat his back, stroke his hair. You can make it clear that it's loving—rather than lovemaking—that's being offered.

Worth Practicing

There is also, of course, a lot to be said for the kind of touching that helps to put you and your husband in a mood to make love.

Developing a sense of touch is one of the very best methods of enhancing sensual technique. Erotic touching must always be feather light. Touch your partner with one finger at a time—lowering a finger, raising it, lowering another, always keeping a finger in contact. Or apply all four fingers (the thumb is usually excluded) in a stroking movement, as gently as possible, lightly grazing your partner's skin. The ideal is a touch so light that the lucky subject can't tell exactly when you begin or stop. This can also be done with the fingernails, although it's harder to keep the touch as feather-light.

It's worth practicing on yourself to get the feather-light touch you want. Touch your own face or thighs until you find exactly the barely perceptible pressure you're looking for. You'll know, because if you're doing it right, the skin will have a tingly excited awareness, as if downy body hairs were rising to meet a lover's caress.

Outdoor and Indoor Magic

I watched a young couple at the beach on a hot day in July. The young man began to rub his girlfriend down with suntan oil, using such lingering delicate movements that it made my mouth dry just to watch. Then he lay prone while she began to work on him. Suddenly I noticed Bill watching with the same intense silent admiration that I'd been displaying. Those two weren't just putting suntan oil on each other. They were practicing the art of erotic massage.

After about ten minutes, Bill and I decided we'd better go for a swim just to cool off. The water was cold that day, so we weren't gone more than a few minutes. When we returned the young couple was walking off together, holding each other so close they kept bumping into each other as they moved. They were heading toward the parking lot. I'll give you odds forever that they didn't even wait until they got the car out of the lot. When two young healthy people are in *that* mood, they take advantage of any occasion—and any place.

Nivea cream or plain cold cream or baby oil can work the same magic indoors. All you need is something to lubricate the movement of hands on skin. You could even use machine oil (if it only didn't smell like machine oil) and get the same results.

Erogenous zones are overrated. Some parts of the body, especially the genitals, are acknowledged to be more sensitive than others. But part of the reason may be because they so rarely are touched. The art of languorous stroking and massaging and touching has been practiced since the days of the ancient Greek courtesans and without any helpful hints from books. On almost any part of the body, the right touch is a turn-on, the wrong touch is a turn-off, and nothing is neurotic that is erotic. There, in a nutshell, is all you need to know about erogenous zones.

Playing A Role

Prudery is a no-no. What's more, it always was a no-no. If you really are a prude, you're cheating yourself of a lot of fun. And you're probably deceiving yourself about your real feelings.

If you could enter the mind of the most uninhibited sexual libertarian for a while, you'd probably find nothing there that hasn't passed through your own mind at some time or other. The erotic fantasies of the most rigid and repressed among us are often as colorful—and often kinkier—than the most uninhibited.

Remember, nobody can arrest you for what you're thinking. No one can even find out unless you tell them. More and more women *have* been telling us lately, from Erica Jong to Gael Greene to the unidentified women who offer their wildest sexual fantasies to the authors of magazine articles or best-selling books.

Not that there aren't plenty of women still playing a role that was in vogue a generation ago, pretending to be shocked or offended if the conversation turns slightly blue or if someone drops one of those unmentionable four-letter words. These same women may have scribbled graffiti on the walls of the ladies' room when they were teenagers themselves. They probably had long furtive conversations with their girl friends about s-e-x, or about what boyfriends tried to do and how they felt when boys did it. Or they giggled and sneaked looks at *Playboy*, or hid Dr. Reuben's *Everything You Always Wanted to Know About Sex* inside the cover of *Trigonometry III*.

Today, they drag their husband, lovers, or dates off to see the latest X-rated movie—even though they may have wondered out loud about what kind of people go to see such films. For the most part, *they* are the people who go to see such films.

Training Films

Well and good. Hypocrisy is as American as apple pie. But if you're the kind of woman described above, just be sure that your fake prudery doesn't carry over into the bedroom. That is not the place for it. Nor is it the place to act as if you're a scared little girl, or Snow White, or a helpless white body in the clutches of King Kong. Instead, recall some of the libidinous thoughts that have actually occupied your mind at odd hours, or some of the things you've dreamed about. That will help to remove your inhibitions.

Suppose you're with your husband making love, and there is something you wish he would do to you. But you feel you can't ask him to do it, because asking isn't romantic.

There are some situations in which asking then

and there is the best—and most romantic—idea. But there are many husbands who might construe any suggestion as criticism of their lovemaking. In that event, wait for a better time and occasion, and bring up the subject casually. Sensual pleasure is a process of accommodation. He should want to please you as much as you want to be pleased, but the approach shouldn't involve personal criticism. You might say you'd read about a certain technique somewhere and would like to try it. He'll probably be pleased that you were thinking about making love with him, and therefore more receptive to the idea of making your lovemaking even better.

If inspiration fails you, by all means take a refresher course. Most X-rated movies are, at the least, instructive, and they may start your sensual juices flowing. Think of them not as dirty movies but as training films. Many women find that it's a pleasant way to learn.

Some women don't want to learn. Emily, for instance, told me, "My husband says that when it comes to sex, anything goes. But I don't enjoy his abnormal tastes. I'd like to let him know how I feel without turning him off completely."

Well, everyone has a different idea about what is "normal"—especially concerning sex. Some people greatly enjoy the same activities that others find abhorrent. One person's fish is another's *poisson*. I told Emily she might begin by examining her own attitudes. Did she equate certain sexual practices with being "bad" or "evil" or "licentious?" She had had the kind of upbringing that taught her to repress certain feelings, or condemn them. But it *is* possible to reeducate oneself. Many women think that a headache is a good way to avoid sex. The way I look at it, sex is a good way to avoid headaches.

In marriage, if you want a mutually enjoyable sex life (and you'd better!), you can't afford to be rigid and inflexible. If, for example, some sexual activity gives your husband a great deal of pleasure but leaves you cold—though not repelled—why not do it because you love him and want to please him?

Something Borrowed, Usually Blue

Let's talk about the kind of explicit fantasies in which you lie abed imagining what some man is doing to you. In adolescence, the men who visited you in your fantasy life were masked or otherwise faceless. Their identity didn't matter. What they were doing to *you* is what mattered. There's hardly a woman alive who doesn't remember her rape fantasies. The authors of the popular "rape sagas" are just putting down in story form what women have been harboring in their heated imaginations for a long time.

In the old days, popular historical romances and gothic novels took the reader to the door of the bedroom just as the chapter ended. What happened between the end of that chapter and the beginning of the next was left to the reader's imagination. Often that still is true, for the technique was a sound one: almost any woman can supply all the titillating details from her own fantasies stored up over the years.

The newer tempestuous romances, on the other hand, carry the audience right over the threshold of the bedroom door. The chapter doesn't end until the last contortion and groan. It may be that this trend will eventually erode our ability to fantasize, though somehow I doubt it.

You don't even need imagination to fantasize. Let yourself go. Rule out any criticism of what you're thinking, even if it turns out to be as amusingly impractical as Woody Allen's fantasy of being smothered to death in Italian actresses. And if you can't let yourself go because of deep-seated inhibitions, borrow someone else's fantasies. There's a whole literature on the subject. Nobody's going to sue you for plagiarism.

If you fantasize that Robert Redford is stepping unexpectedly into your bedroom at midnight, wearing a T-shirt and an alarming erection, that doesn't mean you're bored or dissatisfied with your husband. Nor does a fantasy of rape mean that in real life you want to be raped. The fantasy of a woman making love to you does not mean you're a lesbian. The fantasy of being at an orgy where lots of men are doing all kinds of things to you does not mean you'd enjoy a real-life orgy.

That's the marvelous thing about fantasies. They have nothing to do with reality. But you can borrow a little something from them, and put *that* into real life. This is a normal, healthy way of adding excitement to lovemaking. The fact that you're making use of a mental aphrodisiac signifies that your marriage and your sexuality are being fueled by a wholesome imagination.

There are a great many women who need the fuel of fantasy to maintain their natural sex drive. At least one survey has shown that women who fantasize during lovemaking tend to enjoy sex more, and that wives who do are more likely to be satisfied with their marriages. According to this survey, women whose thoughts *never* stray tend to be repressed and less able to enjoy making love than their more imaginative sisters.

Of course, surveys are always to be taken with several large grains of common sense. Surveys deal with statistics, and you are *not* a statistic. Women who do not fantasize while making love are neither "out of it" nor substandard lovers. If a survey showed that most women preferred string beans to asparagus, this should not make asparagus-fanciers feel inferior.

Take, for example, my good friend Renée, who told me the other day, "I have a wild fantasy life, but when I'm making love I'm so turned on by my partner that I don't think of fantasizing—though I may initiate or suggest something whose roots are in my fantasy."

On the other hand, if you would like to become a more active sensual fantasizer, what can you do about it?

The First Time

Let's go back to the very beginning again, shortly after you and your husband first met. No question then about who inhabited your fantasies while you were lolling in the bathtub. *He* was your dream lover. He usurped the place of all those mythical masked or naked men who had once galloped across your private erotic movie screen.

If that's changed, there's an easy way to put him back in the picture. Even if your sexual relations lately haven't been the kind that would set anyone to daydreaming, you have memories to work with. Use them. Forget the boring present—if that's how you think of it—and focus your thoughts on the more exciting moments in your relationship.

Reconstruct the very first time you made love, just as it happened. If the first time was something short of incendiary, substitute the first *good* time. Put it into the precise setting. Now imagine a clock on a table and set its hand for the beginning of this scene. Minute by minute, live through the experience again. Don't skip anything. If you're tempted to, look at the clock again. The hands aren't speeding ahead. Only a few minutes have elapsed. Ask yourself: What are you doing now? What did you say? What did he say? Are no words being spoken? What were you wearing when you began to undress or when he was undressing you? What was he wearing? Go right through the experience in minute detail, leaving out nothing, until you are finally full of the sensual sweetness of that very first time.

Do the same thing with other recollections simmering on the back burner of your mind. That time you took a bath together, soaping and touching each other.

Turning On

That picnic on a perfect spring day: You may not remember what you packed in the picnic hamper, but you haven't forgotten the impulse that sent you both off into the woods. Remember how the interlacing branches and leaves looked over your head, and how the grass smelled? You need as many details as possible in order to summon back and fix the experience firmly in your mind and savor it. These examples may not be out of your particular bag of memories, but you have had your own unforgettable occasions—mornings, afternoons, evenings.

The power of recall knows no statute of limitations. You can recapture the sights, sounds, smells, taste and touch of many a languorous interlude with your mate. That's the stuff dreams are made of. And dreams are the stuff that makes a marriage endure.

Creating the Environment

To the older generation of women, romance is something that happens in some exotic locale with Clark Gable or Charles Boyer or Robert Taylor. Romance has very little to do with marriage.

To the middle aging generation, romance is something that is an interesting *prelude* to marriage. The locale does not have to be exotic. After marriage they settle down to live in the real world, ever after. After marriage, romance dies.

To the younger generation, romance may be something that never existed except in the minds of the older generations.

All three interpretations are mistaken. Romance does not have to take place on a gilded barge sailing down the Nile. That barge sank a long time ago. Those who limit the romantic to the exotic are missing the boat.

Nor is romance merely a prelude to marriage; it is an aura that, with a little effort, can be made to endure all the years of your married life. As the poems and novels illustrate, and the wisest philosophers assure us, romance has always been with us—thousands of years before the younger generation decided to vote it out of existence in favor of open, "natural," sex.

Romance exists. And it begins at home.

By "home" I am not talking about San Simeon or the cloud-capped towers of fantasy. I'm talking about *your* home. Stop pursuing the impossible dream long enough to see the very possible happiness that is here for the taking in your apartment, house or houseboat, anyplace where your marriage happens.

Among the many factors that go into a honey-moon-marriage, environment ranks high. Your environment is your home, so become an environmentalist.

Redecorating Your Marriage

The way you and your husband react and interact in this environment has more to do with the quality of your marriage than you might think. Your home has the power to lift your spirits or drop them in the dust, to make the world seem cheery, comfortable and cozy or turn it into a place of stygian gloom.

The home also has the power to increase your sensual appreciation of each other.

Georgianna and David were newlyweds when I first knew them. Anyone would have spotted them as one of those lucky couples destined to be long-and-happily married. They moved into David's fourth-story walk-up apartment. But after a while—it took longer than I would have thought—they began to be dissatisfied with their love nest. It was charming but too small, and walking up those four flights, especially when carrying heavy grocery bags, was too much. They found a large apartment on the second floor of a building that fronted on a busy street. They had to buy the previous tenant's furniture to get the apartment, and the previous tenant's taste ran the gamut from dismal to dolorous. The apartment was close to the street, and surrounding buildings shut out the light, which offered them all the benefit of street noise and living in the twilight zone.

One day at lunch, Georgianna told me, close to tears, that their sex life had dwindled to almost nothing.

"We still love each other," she told me, "but everything is going to pieces. I just don't see how it's possible for two people to carp at each other all the time like we do and still enjoy being married. What am I going to do?"

"Have you thought about redecorating?"

Georgianna looked at me as if I were making some sort of cruel joke.

"I'm serious," I assured her. "Frankly, I think your

apartment is one of the dreariest I've seen. It depresses *me*, and I only see it occasionally. It could be having much the same effect on you and David."

"We can't afford to throw the furniture out. We paid too much for it. We're stuck with it."

"You can still try to make everything brighter and cheerier. The way your home looks doesn't just affect how *you* feel—it also sends the wrong message to David. It says you don't care about his comfort, or your own. If a home is inviting, you're inviting him in. He feels welcome and wanted."

Georgianna took the advice to heart. A few weeks later, Bill and I were invited to dinner at their redecorated apartment. Everything looked much brighter, thanks to new fabrics, mirrors, colorful wall hangings, and pretty draperies. When I complimented her, David broke in enthusiastically. "She did it on a shoestring. Isn't she amazing? What beats me is that the place doesn't have that overdecorated look I hate. I like to relax in my own home and not sit around nervous and wondering if I'm messing anything up. This place is just perfect."

At my next lunch with Georgianna, I wasn't surprised to hear that the marriage had improved as much as the apartment. "David and I couldn't be happier," she said. "But I still can't get it through my head that solving our problem was as simple a matter as brightening up our surroundings."

"You did more than that," I told her. "You opened the doors and gave romance a chance to come in. You sent him a message of love."

I don't mean to imply that love can't take place in a garret, or that passion will fray around the edges as soon as your sofa does. It's entirely a question of what emotional message is being sent—and received.

Clutter and Mrs. Craig

Craig's Wife, a play later made into a movie starring Joan Crawford, featured a woman who put so much store in her house and furnishings that she ended up losing her husband. There are more women like that than you can shake a dust mop at. Ironically, Joan Crawford was like that herself. She kept the furniture in her magnificent living room covered in plastic—no one was allowed to sit comfortably in her expensive chairs. Her compulsive neatness may have been one reason she had a lonely time of it during her last years.

I never knew Joan Crawford, but I know many women like Clara, a "perfect housekeeper" who hates clutter with a passion. Her home is always immaculate. That environment is sending a message to her husband: "This is *my* showplace; I don't really have a place for you in it. Admire what I've done, but please don't use it too much. Hands off!"

The other extreme is equally to be avoided. Perpetual clutter is the accumulation of years, and carries the same wrong emotional message to your husband: There is no room here for you. You are saying, in effect, I'd rather have another piece of bric-a-brac than leave space for you to sit and read your paper or to put up your feet.

Furniture and Your Love Life

Furniture and its arrangement dictates in part the kind of life you are going to lead. If your living room is full of deep armchairs with strategically positioned bright reading lights, then you are going to do a lot of reading. If the chairs and sofa face the stereo set, and you have a prominent pair of expensive speakers, and your records are all easily accessible, you are going to do a lot of listening to music. If the most comfortable places to sit all face the television set, which happens to be prominently situated in the living room, then sure as the next commercial, you'll spend a lot of your time watching TV.

I realize that living habits more often dictate the way furniture is arranged than vice versa, but I'm not putting the coach before the horse. I'm just pointing out that the furniture arrangement also indicates—and, to a degree, controls—the kind of life you *want* to have. Putting a man down on a sunny beach will lead to swimming, and putting him near a snowy slope will invite skiing, and the way you plan the arrangement and the decorating in your home will also lead to certain kinds of activity.

The chief room to think about when you consider creating that environment is the bedroom. It is, by far, the most important room in your house. Too many married couples aren't aware of its importance in their lives.

Don't be deceived by the fact that you spend more time in the living room, the kitchen, or the family room. You don't measure the quality of living by the number of hours you spend at an activity. If you did, washing dishes would be more important than making love.

A married couple I know lived in a perfectly splendid house on spacious grounds near New Orleans. Their home was furnished with lovely antiques, fascinating curios, and beautiful—but comfortable— furniture. The bedroom, however, had an almost spartan look. Two twin beds were set at opposite ends of the room, a dresser in between. The draperies were beige, the bedspreads were beige, and the walls were totally bare except for a small mirror over the dresser.

I was sorry to hear—though I can't say I was surprised—that my New Orleans friends are now in the process of getting a divorce. Their lovely home is up for sale. I only hope the next occupants will be a little wiser.

Wives usually choose the bedroom decor, but that doesn't mean the room should be all frills and femininity. That's just another way of telling a husband he's an intruder. When decorating the bedroom, take into account his sensibilities as well as yours.

Heightening the Drama

Here are a few practical tips:

There's nothing like two, three, or more artfully positioned mirrors to suggest that a bedroom is a place that's more than just for sleeping in. Mirrors carry a psychological message: what goes on here is worth reflecting or viewing from several different angles. A mirror is also a way of expanding the dimensions of a room—and of an experience.

We've all read about or seen photographs or movie recreations of fancy brothels with plush red velvet draperies and mirrors on the ceiling. Not too many of us would go that far in the way of bedroom decoration, although I'm not going to criticize a woman who tries. (She may have realized that her conventional husband is really an exhibitionist at heart.)

Most of us can be more discreet and get the same effect. No one else has to know about the mirror inside the closet door that, when opened at just the right angle, gives an interesting view of the bed. The side panels of the three-paned dressing table mirror can also be adjusted to encourage provocative glimpses. And no one will guess that the long horizontal mirror stretching across your double dresser was put there because it provides a cinemascope view of the bed.

Then there are mirrored tiles. They are easy to put up, and you can do a wall in almost no time—just for an artistic effect, naturally! (It *is* true that, from a decorating standpoint, you'll make your bedroom look twice as big.)

Your husband may tease you about your efforts, but he's likely to be flattered that you take his lovemaking seriously enough to want to give it the best possible setting. Once he tests out your dramatic new additions, he'll get into the swing of things.

Speaking of dramatic new effects, don't overlook the lighting. You can do more, much more, with lights than with furniture. A Hollywood director or cameraman will take hours to set up exactly the right lighting—and they know what they're doing. A bare little section of a room—sometimes a mere table and chair—suddenly takes on an entirely new dramatic appearance.

Conversely, if you lit the grand ballroom of Versailles palace with bare unshaded light bulbs, it would probably look like a large warehouse in which some garish-looking furniture was being displayed. But when the great chandeliers are dripping lights, and the cleverly concealed spotlights and the gorgeous lamps are casting their magic spells, the ballroom becomes a magnificent showplace.

You don't need an electrical engineer to wire your bedroom for a sight-and-sound spectacular. All you need is the right placement of lamps—with perhaps one spotlight for a little extra pizazz—and an assortment of tinted bulbs. With these, you can transform your ordinary, uninviting, or even frumpy bedroom into passion's hideaway. If you put a pink- or red-tinted bulb or two in lamps, your familiar bedroom will take on a whole new aura. You might enjoy imagining yourself in one of those fancy New Orleans bordellos. You're the loveliest Lorelei ever in waiting, and your husband is a millionaire robber baron with an unslakable thirst for your body. Pink-tinted lightbulbs mellow the mood—and do wonders for your skin.

For the ultimate in romance, fall back on that favorite lighting of old, the kind that lured lovers on to ecstasy long before Edison. Yes, I do mean candlelight.

There is hardly anyone whose face doesn't improve when lit by candlelight, and the light has an especially flattering effect on the nude human body. Skin becomes lambent and glowing, and the flickering flames seem to conceal and reveal at the same time. By all means, get yourself some candles or, if you don't already have one, a candelabra. That handsome, mysterious stranger in the bedroom may turn out to be your husband.

The Best Since Baby Oil

Let's give a little thought to where most of your marital lovemaking will take place: the bed. We spend approximately one-third of our lives sleeping. This does not include the countless hours one spends in bed relaxing, reading, napping, watching television, talking on the telephone, and, of course, making love. Your bed is one item on which you definitely should not stint. Buy the very best mattress you can afford. (The firmer the bed, the better the leverage!) If budget is a problem, get a board to put under the mattress.

As for style, there are all kinds to choose from: twin-size, double, queen and king, platform, four-poster, sleigh-beds, and waterbeds. Your choice will be dictated by your preference, lifestyle, and decorating scheme. But give some thought to how your choice of bed will influence your love life.

If you are devoted to twin beds, consider the European custom of pushing them together and having night tables on both sides of the joined beds. This decorating style encourages intimacy (sexual and otherwise), while still giving you the comfort of separate mattresses. Two twin beds pushed together are exactly the size of one king-size bed—so, if you like the look, find yourself a beautiful king-size bedspread and treat your two beds (outwardly) as one.

However, many couples (Bill and I included) who once thought they preferred twin beds in order to get better sleep, have discovered the joys of owning a king-size bed. A bed this large allows plenty of room to sleep in without bumping each other—in fact, you may have to make a concerted effort even to find each other! Also, its mega-size is conducive to lots of variety in lovemaking. Bill and I recently purchased a super-firm king-size bed; I adore its comfort and luxurious roominess, and when I'm particularly bone-weary, have been known to murmur a grateful "thank you" for it as I crawl in.

Then there are the waterbed devotees. I know couples who swear that a waterbed is the best aid to sex since baby oil, that there is nothing on earth like its sensual wave-like motion when wife and husband also happen to be in motion. As for sleeping, they say it cradles you as gently as amniotic fluid.

Waterbeds have been on the market long enough so that today's models are better made and less expensive than they used to be. They cost no more than a good mattress and box spring, and—contrary to scare stories you may have heard—they don't leak or explode or create tidal waves. They can't get lumpy, and you won't be distracted by the squeaking and groaning of bedsprings, which do protest when sexual gymnastics get at all strenuous. However, don't plunge into aquatic sleeping gear without investigating the pros and cons. I personally would be afraid of seasickness every time I'd lie down, and I have heard of couples who loved their water bed at first but before long grew to hate it.

Whatever type and style of bed you choose, keep in mind that it is *important*. It is worth careful thought, and the money you spend on it is wisely invested.

A Fine and Private Place

Nothing inhibits sensual enjoyment quite as much as extraneous noises, particularly when the noises are a by-product of the activity. A couple can complete a sex act despite barking dogs, squealing car brakes, even the shrieks and giggles of children at play. What's far more likely to disturb their concentration is a squeaky bed's counterpoint to each movement, or a headboard's rattling against a wall.

One friend of mine was so disturbed by the sounds that went along with coupling in her bed that she wore earplugs. "They're as necessary as my diaphragm," she told me. A new bed strikes me as a better solution. Earplugs or not, she had to be aware that her two children might overhear the noises and interpret them correctly. Not that this is necessarily bad for the children, but the idea *can* be disquieting to the parents. If you're the kind of mother who keeps her children away from R-rated movies, you won't be too comfortable providing them with X-rated home entertainment.

There are steps you can take to secure privacy for your most intimate moments. If your bed is against a shared wall, move it to a "safe" wall. Try to ensure that the bed is squeakproof. If the headboard rattles, or bangs against the wall, carpet the side that's against the wall. That will sharply reduce the sound (and, as a fringe benefit, will also keep the headboard from making scuff marks on the wall).

Furnish your bedroom with draperies and heavy pile rugs that absorb sound. These have additional advantages: The draperies keep out chinks of light and the rugs are luxurious to walk on. If you have a thick, deep-piled rug, you may dispense with the bed altogether on occasion. Change of scenery usually perks up a jaded sexual appetite—and a floor offers better leverage than even the firmest orthopedic mattress.

I am not, of course, suggesting that you turn your bedroom into a tomb. A tomb's a fine and private place, to paraphrase the poet, but not for those who would embrace. What I am suggesting is that you make your bedroom into a private sanctuary in which you and your husband can indulge the urge to merge whenever you wish.

The Road to Emerald City

If other people live in your house or apartment, and that includes little people, it's essential to establish and enforce certain ground rules. Your bedroom should be a refuge at any hour of the day or night. When your bedroom door is closed, no one—but no one—should be allowed to intrude. Lock your door. Insist that family members knock. There will be times of emergency—and to a four-year-old having a nightmare is an emergency. But children can learn that a closed bedroom door means Keep Out.

Most of the time, it isn't likely you'll be doing anything more exciting in the bedroom when the door is closed than lolling abed watching television or reading. The important thing to get across is that when the door is closed, you are to be left undisturbed if at all possible. It's important that you and your husband be able to relax and enjoy yourselves in your bedroom-sanctuary.

As I hope I've made clear by now, I don't consider sex and sensuality to be identical. Keep that distinction firmly in mind. For example, nothing is quite so comforting as a Sunday breakfast *a deux*, with newspapers scattered on the counterpane and your favorite music on the radio. Saturday morning can also be a fine time for privacy, because small children are likely to be glued to the television set.

All you need is a breakfast tray, the newspapers, and music to know what Omar Khayyam was talking about when he wrote, "A jug of wine, a loaf of bread, and thou singing beside me in the wilderness. Ah, wilderness was paradise enow!" Standards change, and wine and bread may strike you as a less than ideal breakfast, and there aren't too many wives who'd be thrilled by their husbands singing, even in the shower. But the principle is the same. A few creature comforts, someone you love near you, and you're on the road to Emerald City.

The bedroom can be a place to talk and dream, as well as to have sex. A woman I interviewed for this book told me she keeps travel brochures and her journals of past travels in a drawer of her night table, along with a photo album record of every trip she's taken with her husband.

"You'd be surprised how much fun it is to relive the marvelous times of your life," she said. "It's almost as much fun as going in the first place."

Recalling the happy times you've had with your husband, like dreaming together about times to come, can make the two of you feel particularly close. And after all, trips into the past—or the future—cost you nothing.

When you're in the mood, any place is a good

place for making love. Your living room should certainly not be limited to entertaining and family gatherings. Don't overlook the possibilities of the rug in front of the fireplace. And an attractive wide sofa, comfortable and pillowed, makes an inviting change of place for lovemaking.

One of our friends told Bill that some of the very best encounters he has with his wife are in the closet. They just pop in out of sight, and curl up on the floor. Or they stand up amid the coathangers and clothing. He said he particularly likes it in his wife's closet ("the feeling of all those silky, taffety, feminine things around really turns me on"), but in a pinch any old closet will do. There is something about the "claustrophobic intimacy" that he—and, apparently, she—finds exciting. I haven't gotten around to testing this myself yet (I've got a dozen unexplored locations of my own to visit with Bill first), so I pass it on without recommendation. The point is that no place need be declared out of bounds. One of my most memorable experiences was sitting on top of the washing machine while the clothes were churning underneath. Talk about dual action!

Water Trysts

The aphrodisiac qualities of water have long been known. Among the kinds of erotic fun you can have in the bathroom is giving your husband a bath.

First, let's pay a little attention to the environment. Make sure your bathroom does not send out the wrong vibrations. A messy bathroom does. So does a brightly lit bathroom with light gleaming off the tiles and stark white walls. A police interrogation is properly conducted under strong direct white light, but no one has ever praised a police interrogation for its sensuality.

I don't mean you have to completely redo your bathroom. But you can replace the bulbs in the light fixture with ones that shed a soft, inviting light. And if you want to go all-out for special (sensual) occasions, dispense with electric light altogether and use candles. The flickering of candlelight on walls duplicates the gentle shimmer of water in the tub.

Other redecorating tips: Don't put skimpy towels on the rack. Small towels give the message of economy, not luxury, and you want the feeling of a small room wrapped in deep pile. Have handy not only your own beauty-bath products, but also bath powders and masculine scents that your husband will enjoy using. You might also consider spraying the bathroom with a light fragrance. A woman's favorite scent in the air is a turn-on for most men, and puts her more intensely into the picture. However, some men don't like to be surrounded by a feminine scent. He may like the fragrance on you but not in the air. If that's the case, use a masculine scent or a "neutral" one, like cinnamon or patchouli.

Obviously, the purpose of giving your husband a bath is not just to get him squeaky clean. You can even omit soap. What you're looking for is sheer relaxation with fun to follow.

By all means, help him get ready for the sensual dunking. Undress him. And remember, you're not undressing a male mannequin in a store window. Pleasure, not efficiency, is the name of this game.

I'll have more to say on this and other forms of water sports in the next chapter on Having Fun, but here I'm chiefly concerned with creating the right environment in the bathroom. It may be the smallest room in your house, but sensually it's among the most important.

A final word. Some women have told me that they only really share a sensual atmosphere with their husbands when they're on vacation. At home, no matter how comfortable or inviting their surroundings, they always seem to be picking at each other and discontented.

It may simply be that outside problems intrude themselves at home. Children may be underfoot, business problems may be harassing your husband, and because you're both tired you may not have the energy and willingness to meet each other's needs. An obvious solution is to parallel, as closely as you can, the conditions that prevail on vacation. I know you can't banish the children, and your husband can't quit his job, and you can't neglect the house. But try to bear in mind that duty does not always come before pleasure. No matter how crowded your schedule, you can allow more time for rest and play. Children can look after themselves better than you think, work problems don't always have to travel home with your husband from the office, your house does't have to be as clean as a laboratory. Sensual pleasure should have equal priority with work on your schedule, and, in the happiest households, will usually rank first.

Having Fun

For one couple I knew, fun time in their marriage came when the kids were asleep and they were alone in the privacy of their bedroom. They put their favorite music on the record player. They took off their clothes.

And they danced.

Something about their nakedness, and about the fact that they were doing something most people simply don't do, made the experience marvelously sensual for them. Often they danced together for an hour, then went to bed without any need to have sex—but feeling close to each other, and loving.

There is no reason why sensuality should be a solemn affair. Richard Burton, an accomplished lover who has had love affairs with a score of the most beautiful women in the world, once said the quality he valued most highly in a woman was the ability to make playful love, to "laugh in bed."

Sensual game-playing can be fun. All you need is a little imagination.

Let's say you're at a large gathering, a wedding reception perhaps, or a dance. You and your husband can play Strangers. It's easy. All you have to do is pretend that this is the first time you're seeing each other. Both of you act smitten at first glance. You can begin with some serious flirting. Make your glances at him intense, inviting. Smolder. When he comes over to you, act as though your emotions are in chaos and you can hardly get your breath for a minute.

Silly? Of course, that's part of the fun.

You're also honing up your sensuality while you're playing the game. Though it's only make-believe, you appear to each other in a new, attractive guise. Bill and I have played Strangers on occasion at large social affairs where everything was so boring we could have cut our throats just to have something to talk about. The game of pretending to be love-smitten strangers helps pass the time agreeably.

There are all sorts of variations on the game. I went shopping for Bill's birthday present in a men's store in Manhattan, and he agreed to meet me there in half an hour. I picked out a good-looking blazer for him. When Bill showed up he pretended not to know me, so I knew the game was afoot. I wondered aloud to the salesman whether the blazer I had chosen would fit my husband; I described him as six-foot-three, two hundred pounds, well proportioned. Then I "suddenly" noticed the stranger looking through a rack nearby. "Why, he's almost exactly my husband's size!" I said. "Could you ask him to try it on?" The salesman demurred politely, so I went over and asked for myself.

Bill, playing his role, was all courtesy and willingness to help. He tried on the blazer, which of course fit perfectly. Then he tried on a shaggy tweed jacket for me. Now the two of us began making rather obvious progress toward becoming friends. I noticed the salesman giving us slightly questioning glances. Finally, I decided on the blazer. "Since you look so marvelous in it," I told Bill, "I'm sure it will look well on my husband too." He invited me to lunch. Taking his arm, I gracefully accepted the invitation. As we left, Bill said in a tone that the salesman could overhear, "And perhaps later you could come to my place. I have a new George Bellows lithograph I'd like to show you."

The salesman had a good story to tell his wife that night, and Bill and I had a good laugh over lunch. And I told him, "You really did look wonderful in that blazer. Sometimes I forget what a madly attractive husband I have!"

A Great Romance

Seeing your husband as a stranger again for a little while often reminds you of why you were attracted to him in the first place.

Vivian and Archer, married 14 years, went us one better. Boarding ship for a cruise to the West Indies, they noticed about 20 females to every eligible man. Vivian worked out a scenario with Archer. At the first get-together party and dance, they pretended not to know each other. Archer, an attractive man, soon had a whole circle of admiring females around him. As the orchestra was about to strike up for the first dance, Vivian passed by. Archer acted like young Michael Corleone in *The Godfather* the first moment he saw the beautiful Sicilian peasant girl.

Vivian and Archer danced every dance that night, and of course during the cruise had every meal together at a table for two. Other passengers who saw them cuddling in the deck chairs by day, kissing in the shadow of the lifeboats at night, sharing post-midnight cognacs at the bar, thought they were watching the development of a Great Romance. One couple, whom they'd seen often on the cruise, met them coming out of their room on B-deck early one morning. The man and his wife politely averted their eyes and went by without a word.

A year later, Vivian and Archer met this same couple by accident at a Manhattan restaurant and confessed the truth. Both wife and husband were amused—and disappointed. A few days later, Vivian and Archer received a small package of Kodachrome slides in the mail. The couple had been taking surreptitious photographs of them because the Great Romance had been the most interesting feature of their trip. Now that they knew the truth, they'd lost interest in showing the slides!

Surprise!

There are all sorts of sensual games that married couples can, and often should, play. At the very least, playing will add variety, humor—and a little spice—to their relationship. A stunning young woman I know likes to play the role of a wanton in the grip of a dominating passion—for her husband. She will call him at the office and announce, in her sultriest tones, "This is Desirée—I must have your body!" She sends him passionate letters written in scarlet ink on lavender paper, reeking of perfume. One afternoon, she drove by to pick up her husband at his office for a dinner date. She parked in front of his building, but he was late coming downstairs. She lay back on the front seat of the car, positioned her dress partway up her legs, and became Desirée—the very picture of languid seductiveness—waiting for him to open the door.

When he did, he was with a business associate!

"It took a while to straighten that out," she told me, "and I'm still not sure the man is convinced. When my husband and I remember the look on his face, we break up all over again. So maybe it all worked out for the best!"

Reading For Pleasure

Many best sellers these days contain some fairly torrid scenes. This can be a turn-on for you—if you're willing to enact what the author is describing. The acting out of a role so far from your ordinary self is usually a liberating experience. This also works well with soft- and hard-core pornographic books, although these books are usually written by men to turn on men. The writing is awful, to be sure, but who cares? This isn't your hour in English Lit but a post-graduate lesson in how to increase sensuality in your marriage.

"I buy a handful of porno books at a store on Santa Monica Boulevard that specializes in the stuff," says Diane, who is married to Leslie, an electronics engineer. "When Leslie comes home keyed up from the day's work, I sit him down in his favorite armchair with a pitcher full of ice-cold dry martinis, and read a nice juicy porno passage to him. After a while, he gets very mellow. At that point, I close the book, and we go into the bedroom where I act out what I've just read. I've never had to say 'Aaaah!' so many times—unless it was to my dentist or doctor!"

Another way of having sensual fun is to subscribe to *Playboy* and *Penthouse*. Posing as the girls do in each issue is sure to titillate. "It's like having my own pet or playmate at home," one husband explained. "My wife reads to me aloud those things the girls are supposed to have said that accompany the photos. I know the quotes are mostly made up by the interviewers, but what's the difference? It captures a free-and-easy attitude toward sex that I find very stimulating."

Reading books and magazines that are designed to attract men is also an excellent way of keeping in touch with the kinds of things your man considers sexy. He might be embarrassed to try to do any of those things seriously, but he won't raise any objection if you find a way to do it that's all in fun.

Pass Go—and Collect

Here's a way of having sensual fun that serves two other purposes as well. Let's assume that you've entertained fantasies of being one—or several—different types of women from the type you are, and let's assume that your husband has fantasies of bedding down with a lot of other women. All right, then: *be* a lot of other women. A cowgirl, a bordello madam, a lingerie model, a bespectacled stenographer with her hair up (who takes off her glasses and lets down her hair at the right moment, just like they used to do in the old movies), a sexy waitress, a bathing beauty (wear your skimpiest bathing suit), or number one girl in a harem (never settle for number two).

When looking for clues as to what might turn your man on, keep an eye out for what models are wearing in ads that catch his interest, what pages of *Playboy* he lingers over the longest, what women his eyes follow when you're out walking or driving, what screen or TV beauties get his attention. Sometimes, of course, it will be the woman herself. But sometimes it will be the way she's dressed—or undressed.

While a costume is a big help, it isn't the be-all and

end-all. Not by any means. For best results, a costume should be combined with other amorous techniques. All in fun, of course.

A woman I met while interviewing for this book told me that her husband had been having lunch at the Playboy Club two or three times a week because he enjoyed watching the pretty waitresses in their Bunny costumes. She went to the manager of the club to try to purchase a costume for herself, but was turned down because the Bunny costume is patented. However, being an ingenious woman, she worked out her own costume—a very reasonable facsimile, using a swimsuit cut low at the neckline and high at the leg with laces up the side of the thigh. To this she added two big shaggy powder puffs sewn together to make a Bunny tail. Bunny ears were made from wire hangers covered with fabric and sewn on a hair clip, and detachable collar and cuffs and a black bowtie were purchased at a gentlemen's haberdashery.

That night, when she showed up in her new outfit, wearing her very highest high-heeled shoes, to serve dinner to her husband, he was predictably over-whelmed. It was not only the costume, however, that sent a message. It was the fact that she had gone to so much effort to please—and seduce—him. They spent a very memorable evening, in which she was able to fulfill all his fantasies about having a Playboy Bunny to call his very own!

A sophisticated, very sexy lady I know, who is married to a South American diplomat, knew she was in for a rough night after her husband had a particularly trying session at the United Nations. She wore her prettiest blouse and skirt to greet him on his return that evening. She was not wearing a bra and the blouse was fairly transparent, but he didn't notice. A bad sign. This is not the sort of effect that Latin men normally overlook. He went right into his study to work on a speech he had to give the next day.

An hour later, she knocked and heard his irritable "Come in!" She opened the door, carrying a tray with a cold bottle of Dom Perignon champagne, chilled glasses, caviar and biscuits, and a small "surprise" box. Her irritable, impatient husband gave her one look, put down pen and paper, took the tray away from her, and took her into his arms to give her a long passionate kiss.

Unusual reaction? Well, possibly I forgot to mention that she had also removed her blouse and was completely naked from the waist up. Later, while they were sipping champagne and nibbling caviar, he became curious about the little "surprise" box. When he opened it, he laughed—at least, that's what he did first. She had bought a package of French ticklers, rather fancily-decorated condoms.

Another woman told me that she and her husband enjoy playing sexy variations on well-known parlor games. In Strip Monopoly, for example, the alternative to paying rent is removing an article of clothing. To keep the game from going on too long, this couple observes another special rule: The first one to pass Go ten times, collects!

Sensual Water

There are endless varieties of fun and games to be had in and around the water.

If you have a swimming pool or a friend with a swimming pool, you may have discovered the voluptuous delight of swimming in the nude. Well, let me tell you that swimming in the nude with your husband is twice as much fun! On a warm night, when only moonlight illuminates the silvery allure of unadorned human bodies turning and gliding in the water, this can be a new experience in sensuality. Combine it with the pleasure of "touching," and you may soon find yourself retreating to the lower end of the pool to explore further possibilities.

As many who have tried it will tell you, the sensation of being half-supported, floating, while making love is one that has few equals—and no superiors.

Of course, this particular water sport can also be tried in the ocean, if the waves aren't too bothersome. If they are, or if you never quite got over the experience of seeing *Jaws I* or *II*, try a lake. I personally find that the excitement of making love in such a wide immensity of water is even more intense than in the confining dimensions of a pool.

An excellent setting in which to sample lubricious pleasures is in a jacuzzi or whirlpool bath. In our apartment complex in southern California, the jacuzzi room was always in use. Apparently every couple in the 178 apartments had discovered the pleasures of dallying in that very warm whirlpool bath. I couldn't blame them. The combined effects of warmth and wetness could tempt anyone beyond their powers of resistance. The first occasion on which Bill and I tried it, an early February morning in 1971, we discovered that Los Angeles had withstood a severe earthquake. Either we never noticed it, or we thought it was us!

For most of us, however, the most easily available opportunity to enjoy the aphrodisial enchantment of water is in our very own shower or bathtub. Let's start from that mundane location and discover some of the lovely sensations that can be had from simply giving your husband a bath.

Enjoy the View

Let's suppose you have undressed him. The last thing you want at this stage is to make him feel the least bit uncomfortable, the subject of an experiment. Once that idea flies into his head, sensuality flies out the window. The advice from here is—*slow and easy*. At each step make him aware that you think his body is marvelously touchable. At the same time, bear in mind that the idea is to create a relaxing, voluptuous interlude—not to build up sexual tension. If he thinks you expect him to perform sexually as a reward for the interlude of pleasure, he can't relax. Make sure he doesn't get that idea. If he does anyhow, well, it's always easy to give in—gracefully.

When he's naked—a self-conscious moment for him unless he's built like Ken Norton—let him know that you think he looks adorable. Even if his physique more closely resembles that of Truman Capote, if you find him attractive in the altogether, you can convince him that you do. If, on the other hand, his nude body turns you off (even when lit by candlelight), forget all about sensual bathing.

Now he's lying in the tub, in water warm enough for his muscles to unwind but not so hot that he's going to uncoil completely and go to sleep. And remember, this isn't a hygienic bath. In Japan, a man will not even get into a tub when he needs a bath. He stands next to it, soaps himself, and rinses off with water that he scoops up from the tub. In that eminently civilized country, the bathroom is separate from the toilet facilities. The bath is circular, and there's a drain in the middle of the floor or along the side to carry the water away. Only when a Japanese man is clean will he get into the tub and begin his bath.

Since we're not in Japan and you probably don't have a circular tub, make do with what you've got. There's your man, relaxing in his tub of deep warming water, and here are you, kneeling by the side of the tub ready to begin underwater massage. You don't want to get your clothes or your negligee wet, do you? So slip out of it. Let him enjoy the view.

Want to really spoil him? Have a nice cold drink at hand—a well-chilled martini, Scotch on the rocks, or a r-r-really cold beer. A glass of apple cider will do just fine if he's a nondrinker. The effect of a cold drink going into his stomach while he's in hot water is what you're after.

Kneeling beside him, start by massaging his legs. Not vigorously, not even with an attempt to knead his oh-so-tired muscles. Just a comforting laying on of hands. You can practically let the water do this kind of massage for you. Cup your hands and slosh water along his skin. Every movement should be leisurely, unhurried. Imagine that you don't want this experience ever to end, and he will get the thought from you. Believe me, he will. There's some controversy about whether it is possible for one person to receive a thought from another mind through the air (telepathy), but the transference of a simple thought through the hands is a demonstrated scientific fact. A simple thought, that is. You can't convey your most secret, complex, deepest emotions or ideas just through your hands—but you probably can't do it any other way either. All you want to get across to him right now is the fact that it would be lovely if this experience extended itself in time, with no fixed ending.

Work up from the ankle to the thigh, and back down, using a caressing touch. You needn't say anything at all. If you do want to talk, tell him in soothing tones how you love the feel of his body under your hands, or remind him of a time on the beach when it was all you could do to keep from running your fingers through his chest hair. (This is a good time to run your fingers through his chest hair.) Add whatever other gently stimulating remarks you can think of that will increase his mood of repose and quiet enjoyment of this haven you've created.

Soft words and a gentle touch are among the best ways anyone has of conveying tenderness, warmth, caring, and that special feeling we call intimacy. Unfortunately, they are rarely used except as a prelude to sex—which limits the bliss of a lovely sensual approach to the comparatively few occasions in which sexual intercourse follows.

Let's get back to your husband, patiently waiting in his bath while I've digressed. By now, he feels as though he's luxuriating in velvet. Skipping over his genital area for the time being, move to the abdomen. Begin massage upward toward his chest, then back down again. Your touch should be as lightly caressing as if you were stroking a fine juicy piece of fruit. Keep adding warm water to the tub from time to time so that the bath temperature stays constant. Not even a change in temperature should disturb this tranquil idyll. He's receiving a marvelous flow of sensory stimuli, and you don't want anything to interrupt the continuing sensations.

You can, of course, vary the sensations a little. You might wear a loofa sponge on one hand while you do the massage. Or, if you have a detachable shower head, detach it and use that as a soothing massage on those parts of his body that lie under a protective film of tub water. The nozzle sprays act like a hundred little questing fingers, giving him a mild tingling sensation through the water.

After the bath? There's plenty of sensual stimulation to be had from a rubdown with the right kind of towels. The rubdown can be either vigorous or languorous.

Then both of you might try lying down on a fluffy rug in front of a crackling fire to sip drinks. I'd suggest champagne, but that's my hangup. You may prefer martinis or brandy or hot tea. If you don't have a fireplace, invest in an electric heater, the horizontal kind that will throw heat along the length of your bodies.

But I've been lingering too long in the bath. There are other possibilities for sensual massage you may have been missing. Including the kind that takes place outside the bath. If you don't have a massage table (why not give him one for Christmas?), any large table will do. Pad it with blankets and a pillow, and choose one that allows you to massage without having to bend over too much. There are advantages, too, to just stretching him out on the rug, with you sitting astride his buttocks or the small of his back. You'll both be nude, which in itself is an effective way of stimulating your partner without hands. But the feeling of your nude body astride him, massaging his shoulders and back and the nape of his neck (a tempting erogenous zone), isn't an experience he's likely to file away under Miscellaneous.

Different Strokes For Different Folks

I probably can't tell you much about vibrators that you don't already know. They have become too familiar to need much discussion. But I would like to mention the resistance some women have to using this kind of artificial stimulation. If not rooted in prudery, it's usually based on the desire to have sex be more spontaneous, more a matter of impulse than calculation.

"When my husband and I are planning a love-in evening," one woman told me, "I hate the idea that he makes so many preparations beforehand. It's bad enough that he keeps a rubbing lotion handy in the night stand next to the bed. Of course, sooner or later the vibrator comes out of the night stand too. I feel like I'm some kind of a mechanical contrivance myself, one that has to be oiled and set in motion."

When I asked if her husband had any objection to being given a vibrator massage, she said the idea of using it on him had never occurred to her. Her attitude suggested that she would consider doing that an affront to her sex appeal—an implication that her charms were not sufficient to stimulate her husband.

She is wrong. Anyone who does not object to touching her husband as a prelude to making love should not object to a vibrator. As a gadget, the vibrator is useless without direction and manipulation by the hand. As long as the hand is propelled by sensual feelings, what objection need there be?

Of course, if you object to vibrators (on whatever grounds) and don't feel like experimenting with them, forget about it. But for those who are interested, I offer two simple tips gleaned from many talks with people who use the vibrator as part of their amatory repertoire.

First, buy a battery-powered model. This enables you to use it anywhere that an impulse may overtake you, rather than confining you to an area that's near an electric power outlet.

Second, get a model that transmits throbbing vibrations to your own fingertips. This kind of vibrator straps onto your hand, leaving your fingers free to do the walking. You don't lose that essential human touch. There are the more familiar models that do the vibrating without needing any help from your fingers, but you're entitled to have some of the fun. Why turn it all over to a machine, which can't appreciate it?

The use of a vibrator is particularly recommended in cases where a man has had difficulty attaining and/or maintaining a full erection. Nothing can erode a man's self-confidence more than this symptom. He associates it with the onset of impotence, the decline of his powers, with growing old, or even the slow approach of death. I'm not kidding. The vital center of male paranoia is located in the penis. If a little work with a vibrator can do anything to prop up a portion of anatomy that props up his self-esteem, why not do it?

The vibrator should be applied to the penis and testicles, the anal area, and the territory that lies between (perineal area). Warning: you're dealing with the most sensitive parts of the male anatomy. They react as keenly to pain as to pleasure, so keep your touch light. He is vulnerable and at your mercy. If you have some secret grudge you'd like to work out, hit a pillow or kick around an old tin can. But stay away from his genital area until you're in the tenderest of moods.

Now he's ready and so are you. With the vibrator on your hand, lightly touch a throbbing finger to his penis and gently move around the corona. Holding his penis gently between thumb and index finger, run your fingers down the whole length of the penile shaft. With a gossamer touch, probe the testicles and the anal-perineal area with your fingertip.

Taking his testicles in the hand that's not holding the vibrator, gently rub your index finger over the exposed surface of the scrotum. Be careful not to let the vibrator bump against this sensitive area.

If he is aroused, place the erect penis flat across the palm of your hand. The vibrator is on the back of your hand. Hold his penis firmly for about 15 seconds while your hand throbs along with his erect penis. By then, it should be able to drive nails into the wall.

If he's not fully aroused by now, check to see if he's breathing.

Love In the Woods

Anna and Joe have been married 29 years. Recently, Joe bought a phonograph record for Anna. They told me I'd never guess what it was, and they were right. It was a recording of music played for the strippers in burlesque houses.

"Have you performed for him yet?" I asked Anna, smiling.

"So far, every night," she told me.

"She's a regular Sherry Britton," Joe said, harking back to a golden era of burlesque—which ended about the time he and Anna were married.

It may sound silly for an older couple to engage in such hijinks, but I've no doubt that Anna and Joe will enjoy their marriage for the rest of their lives.

Thinking of Anna and Joe reminds me of Carol and Eddie, two 60-year-olds who believe that sex gets better after a certain number of years of married life. "When your clock runs down, time doesn't stop," Carol once told me. "Eddie and I believe in keeping our clocks wound up and running, and letting time take care of itself."

Not long ago, they were returning to their home in Connecticut, speeding down the Merritt Parkway.

"You know what I want?" Carol said suddenly. "I want a sou-wester and rubber boots."

"Are you expecting a storm?" Eddie asked.

"I'm going to wear them the next time it rains and I won't wear a stitch underneath. And we'll make love in the woods back of the garden."

Bets and Prizes

I'm not suggesting that you permanently abandon the conventional approaches to love in favor of an endless search for novelty. That would be as bad as the opposite, in which no variety is ever attempted. Making love on a ferris wheel can be exciting once, but it's no way to build a permanent sensual relationship.

During an interview, Arlene told me that at one point she had almost despaired of getting her husband Mike's attention away from sports on television. He worked hard during the week and usually came home too tired to make love. Then, on weekends, he'd climb into the TV set with his six-pack.

"I didn't think there would ever be a way to get close to him unless I worked up an interest in the Mets or the Jets. Then I remembered our minister in church once telling us how the early Christian missionaries converted the heathen in ancient Britain. Instead of asking them to tear down their pagan temples, the missionaries persuaded them to change the form of worship taking place there. The pagan temples remained standing but were converted to churches of God.

"That seemed to me to be a stroke of genius. I made up my mind to use the same basic principle. Instead of fighting with him about watching sports all the time, I could use his interest in sports to get what *I* wanted.

"The next Sunday, Mike settled down in front of the TV set. I'll never forget—it was a game between the Rams and the Buffalo Bills. I suggested that we make a private bet, no money, but the loser had to do *whatever* the other wanted for the rest of the day. I told him, 'You'll have complete control of my body for whatever purpose you want, or vice versa.'

"That intrigued him. He won the bet—and claimed

his prize. I was supposed to be the loser, but I certainly didn't feel like one. I never guessed the kind of sexy things Mike had stored up in his subconscious, including having me serve dinner while I was nude. It certainly was fun finding out!"

The next week they bet on another game, and this time Arlene won. Not surprisingly, they had a marvelous Sunday evening at home. "A couple of weeks later, during a dull game, Mike got so turned on thinking about what he'd do to me later that he couldn't wait for the final score to decide it. We agreed that whatever team was leading at half-time would be the winner. Unfortunately, I won. So I had to wait until the following week to find out what he was so anxious to try. Believe me, the wait was worth it. To tell you the truth, I've even gotten to like football. I'm a dedicated Rams fan!"

The Most Fun Of All

Take a second honeymoon trip. This doesn't have to be as elaborate or expensive as your first honeymoon. Ambiance, timing, and attitude are what's important.

If you approach a trip as "just taking a few days off" or "trying to get away from it all for a little while," you may achieve your objective. But there may not be anything especially sensual about it.

Why not start from the very first suggestion to insure that this will be more than another brief vacation? Which means, don't begin with, "Isn't it time we got away?" or "We need a rest, but where can we go?"

You can also begin directly and simply with, "Darling, you know what I'd really love? I'd love to go on a romantic trip with you!" The concept must be there from the beginning. And this should extend to the planning also. You don't want to go to the same place you might go on an ordinary vacation. You don't need a lot of company or social activity. What you need is privacy. *Alone with you, in a cottage built for two.*

Would you like to return to the scene of the first honeymoon? That involves a risk. You may be tempted to compare the new experience with the old one. Memory, that deceiver, makes comparisons invidious. You may have forgotten any problems, irritations, discomforts, or disappointments during the first honeymoon, remembering it only as an uninterrupted interval of bliss. It is hard to compete with an uninterrupted interval of bliss.

By all means, go as first class as your budget permits. This is your honeymoon, so penny pinching is not in order.

To fully recreate the romantic aura of your first honeymoon, why not have a Second Honeymoon party? Then, like the bride and groom do at a wedding reception, you can steal away while the party is still going on. Your car should be packed and ready to go. If your friends are in the swing of the thing, the car may even bear some legends written in whipped cream, or ribbons tied to the door handles.

Having Fun

Once you're at your trysting place, a cold bottle of your favorite beverage will help the air of festivity. So will a portable tape recorder on which you've taped, in advance, romantic music. Including, of course, "your" song. Most couples have a song that's particularly theirs, that symbolizes their love for each other. Bill and I associate our romantic courtship with "I've Never Been In Love Before." There isn't a touring company of *Guys and Dolls* (the musical in which that lovely ballad was sung for the first time) that doesn't find us sitting front row center.

A symbolic gift is another good idea. One woman friend of mine always chooses a bottle of vintage Moet et Chandon, her favorite French champagne. In our case, it's always been roses. On one of our first dates, Bill arrived bearing two dozen gorgeous long-stemmed American Beauties—to celebrate the fact that it was my 24th birthday. Too many birthdays of mine have passed since for that to be practical any more, if the roses were to keep pace with the years. So we've settled for one perfect red rose to symbolize the event. I never see that rose without being reminded, with deeply tender feelings, of how I felt on the first occasion.

Ridiculously romantic? Sure it is. That's what a Second Honeymoon is all about. And there's no better recipe for heightening sensual feelings between couples in marriage. I know whereof I speak.

It may take a while to win your husband over to some of these ideas for having more sensual fun. Don't rush things, use your own good judgment in picking and choosing, and—above all—don't give up trying. Good things don't always happen with the first attempt. You might be interested to know that Charles Lindbergh had to bail out of a plane on four different occasions before he finally flew the *Spirit of St. Louis* across the Atlantic!

PART
II

DEALING
WITH
PROBLEMS

The Killjoys of Marriage

When a marriage goes wrong, nothing goes right. It is not only difficult to function at a job or to shine socially, it is almost impossible to think about anything else.

Anyone who has lived through that painful experience will not think this description excessive. Most people recover, of course, even if their marriage does not. But the pain is never forgotten—nor is the feeling of a life having gone suddenly, inexplicably, out of control.

For an ailing marriage, one that has something worth salvaging, there is no better cure than Vitamin S—sensuality. Equally important you must try to diagnose what's draining the joy out of your marriage. It's comparatively easy to see what ails someone else's marriage, not so easy to see it in your own. Let's look at some killjoy attitudes that are proving deadly in today's marriages.

The Adoring Wife

Doris was a submissive creature who believed the only way to stay happily married was to agree with her husband on every subject under the sun. Her wifely duty was to accept, admire, understand, forgive, and love her husband without asking anything in return.

If her husband ignored her, she would put up with it; if he bullied her, she would pout briefly and murmur, "Oh, Raymond, sometimes you can be so *mean!*" and hope this would bring him around. She would do anything to avoid offending her lord and master. Never mind that she was a former beauty queen, a college graduate, and had been a highly competent executive in a direct mail order business before marrying Raymond.

That was all in the past. On their honeymoon, in the midst of newly discovered rapture, she had vowed she would devote herself to being Raymond's adoring wife.

After a time, Raymond became convinced that he was the world's most fascinating man, and concluded he was wasting all his magnificence on Doris. She was uninteresting, not at all like the alert, intelligent woman he had married.

And she was getting older, less desirable. She had completed her basic function of giving birth to and rearing their children. Now the children were grown up, or nearly so. Raymond felt he was entitled to a little excitement in his life. Doris was a "good woman," and he would always look after her. But a man like himself—well-to-do, masterful, charming—deserved something more. He left her.

Scarlett O'Hara Speaks Out

Doris was devastated for a time. Then she took stock of herself. She was in her mid-forties, still an attractive woman. She bought a new wardrobe, got a new hairdo, moved to a small apartment which she furnished to her own elegant taste, and she landed a job as an employee in a direct mail business. In two years she was a partner. A year later, she married the man who owned a controlling interest in the business.

Did she do it by playing the totally submissive adoring female? Not on your garterbelt. She won him by becoming the most sensual woman she knew how to be. For the first time in years, she began looking and behaving like a woman.

"The shock of Raymond's leaving me just established the right background for me to become interested in *me* again," she says. "There was another woman involved, naturally, and she was younger. But I never thought she was Raymond's type. She was talkative and she had very strong opinions—qualities Raymond led me to think he hated. She believed in astrology and the occult—areas that Raymond always found laughable. But he found her fascinating. They're married now, and I hope happily.

"What really brought me out of my depression and got me interested in me was the night I picked up *Gone With the Wind* and began leafing through the pages. I came across a passage that riveted my attention. It's Scarlett O'Hara saying how tired she is of acting weak and 'womanly.'

"'I'm tired of saying how wonderful you are to fool men who haven't got one half the sense I've got, and I'm tired of pretending I don't know anything, so men can tell me things and feel important while they're doing it!'

"I decided then and there," Doris says, "to change my ways with the next man I met. I wasn't going to be an adoring, empty-headed, cutesy pie. I wasn't going to coo at men to get them to like me. I was going to use the qualities God gave me as a woman to make an impression. That was all. I didn't have to bow my head, or bind my feet, or walk five paces behind a man to please him. All I had to do was show him that I was an attractive, independent woman with convictions of my own. And with a very healthy interest in an attractive man!"

As a result, Doris had more men flocking around than she knew what to do with. In marriage, her true personality had been as enclosed as a conch shell. As a free-wheeling female, she drew men as effortlessly as a steel magnet draws filings.

Life With A Doormat

The Doormat lacks sensuality because she not only lets her husband walk all over her, she sweeps her sentiments underneath and keeps them hidden. When her husband calls from the train station to say he's bringing home four friends for dinner, she replies in her pleasantest tone, "That's all right, dear. I'll just put on a few more chops for dinner." She then throws out the leftover meal she has prepared and starts over from scratch. When her husband complains later about the money she's spending at the supermarket, she doesn't remind him that she had to buy extra lamb chops—not her. She says she'll try to be more careful about what she spends. Nor does she bring up the fact that the four friends he brought home spilled liquor all over her rug, and she had to spend three hours getting out the stains.

When Doormat makes plans, they are subject to instant revision depending on what her husband would like to do that particular evening. She not only won't make an appointment, she won't express a preference until she's checked with him. When he asks, "What would you like to do this evening?" her answer is, "What would *you* like to do, dear?"

If he launches into a long and boring story that would make anyone else scream, Doormat not only hangs on his every word but now and then, to prove she's been listening, interjects a question that will probably send him off on another interminable harangue.

In the bedroom, Doormat's sex life is governed entirely by her husband's desires, never hers. She never tells him when she isn't in the mood, never suggests anything that might help put her in the mood. Hers is not to question why, or when, or how.

Doormat may claim that her husband absolutely adores her, but the truth is that she has about as much sex appeal as a pet rock.

For some reason lately, the Doormat has been put forward as an ideal by authors whose basic message appears to be that women should be content to spend the rest of their born-again days worshiping their husbands. Their deluded readers keep trying this ridiculous formula for getting along with "their lords and masters." And they find that, even wrapped in cellophane, they are about as attractive as stale bread.

Real love is founded on mutual respect and caring. There may be some men who are only turned on by inferior creatures—but they can't be the majority (or bestiality would be more popular than it is). A real man needs a fully cooperating sensual partner. That means an independent woman interested in the satisfaction of her needs also. Lovemaking is a mutual endeavor—you can't roll a seven with just one die.

Married people should stop thinking of: "who's boss?" The truth is that, in most marriages, neither is confined to the playing of one role. The idea that a woman should always be submissive and a man should always be dominant is as outdated as it is unworkable. At different times a woman can be passive or take a more aggressive role. The same goes for men. The really strong man can afford to be gentle, because he hasn't let himself be trapped into a sexual identity that allows him to do little more than flex his biceps and act self-confident whether he feels that way or not.

Much of the blame for macho men rests with the women who encourage such attitudes. Too many women pretend to be hothouse flowers. Men may admire these frail blossoms but can't be expected to treat them as real persons in or out of the bedroom. If women want to banish the general male conception that they are dependent and passive but also manipulative, that they avoid confrontations while they work slyly behind the scenes, that they feign weakness and vulnerability while actually being strong and demanding—they will have to be more direct and honest.

"I Resented Sharing Him"

There are other attitudes that are equally destructive to a good marriage because they, too, are basically anti-sensual.

Betty, a laboratory technician, married her boss. "Lester and I worked the same hours, usually only a few feet away from each other. We made little signals to each other without anyone else knowing what they meant but us. Then we'd have dinner together, and we made love almost every night. I was on Cloud Nine.

"One day he told me he didn't think it was a good idea for me to work for him at the lab. He said people were talking about him showing favoritism. I was terribly hurt, but I quit. Having to spend the day alone at home, I had to regear my whole life. Taking care of the house didn't occupy me that much. I used to call Lester at the lab on almost any excuse. Finally, he told me not to call him there unless it was for a real emergency.

"A real emergency? I was *entitled* to him. And I resented having to share him with other people, with strangers.

"Finally we had a knock-down, drag-out argument. He told me I was closing in on him more and more, every day. He didn't think he wanted to be married any more.

"I was totally miserable. I'd become completely dependent on him. I didn't know what to do or where to turn. I was at a real low point when I made an effort to pull myself together. I went out and got a job working for a big corporation. The job enhanced my self-image and my economic independence.

"Succeeding at one thing, my job, made a big difference. As a housewife, I'd waited for Lester to come home and entertain me. I'd almost pounced on him the minute he walked in the door.

"My changed attitude changed my marriage. Now it's better than ever. Even sex means a lot more. I used to worry about satisfying him, and even try to rush my orgasm so he wouldn't get bored. Now I relax, enjoy it, and tell him exactly what I like and what I don't. As a result he thinks I'm more sexy and he enjoys making love more.

"I'm not possessive about him because my own ego is healthy. I have good feelings about myself as an individual—and I'll never go back to being a possessive female again!"

Many a woman makes the mistake of thinking that her husband is responsible for her happiness. He is not. *You* are responsible for you. You're the one who has to care about yourself and your own life. If you sit around hoping that your husband will give you a sense of fulfillment, you are in for a great disappointment in marriage.

Jealousy

For some reason, jealousy is often taken to be a proof of love. If it is proof of anything, it is proof of insecurity. Jealousy is an acid that corrodes the bright surface of love and leaves it rutted and pitted with suspicion. All too soon the union is in ruin.

The jealousy, of course, may be his problem, and not founded in your actions. But if you are causing it, you have to take only two steps to bring the situation under control. One: Stop whatever you are doing that gives rise to suspicion. Two: Treat your husband exactly as you would if you were on a honeymoon. Set up every possible situation in which you can be alone together and, when you are, don't let a minute go to waste. A gentle caress, a sudden impulsive kiss, a close press of your body against his, even an admiring glance, will do wonders to restore confidence and to banish the anxiety and suspicion that are closely allied with jealousy. Self-pity and a desire for vengeance, other offshoots of jealousy, can vanish like mist in the morning sun of amorousness. Every sign of love is a sign of reassurance, a statement of sanity that banishes delusion.

On the other hand, if you are the jealous one—even with cause—don't give in to the emotional reactions that all too often accompany jealousy. Hell may have no fury like a woman scorned, but if she can't control her emotions she makes a private hell for herself.

Anita, after only a year of marriage, was thinking of leaving her husband. "I can't trust him. I never feel he loves me as much as I love him. By my standards, he's unfaithful. Every time we go out somewhere I see him giving the eye to other women—and I blow my cool. I can't help it. When I accuse him he denies it, and then we both get mad and days go by without our speaking to each other.

"I can't help being jealous. Unless I can be sure of my man, I don't want to stay married."

On questioning, it became clear that Anita had little evidence to support her jealousy. As a bachelor, Wally had enjoyed the freedom of playing the field. She suspected him of secretly wanting to be that free again. On one occasion, visiting the home of an ex-girlfriend of Wally's who had married someone else, Anita saw him follow her into the kitchen. She followed and, while she didn't actually see them embracing, she was sure they *looked* guilty.

What about the ex-girlfriend's husband, I asked her. Had *he* been suspicious? Anita admitted he was not. Was the other couple happily married? She said they seemed to be. Then, I pointed out, the jealousy all seemed actually to proceed from one source: Anita.

I'm happy to report that Anita, a sensible, intelligent woman, thought it over and finally agreed. At worst, she concluded, Wally's flirtatiousness represented an ego problem of his—and of *hers*—rather than a true gauge of how he felt about her. And her jealousy was keeping her from any possibility of enjoying her marriage.

Getting In Shape

Don't overlook the obvious: check yourself over physically. Do you no longer bear much resemblance to the woman he married? Have you stopped "bothering" with your appearance, except on special occasions? You may have been hearing and reading questions like this until you're sick of them. But face it—if your marriage is showing signs of flabbiness, part of the reason may be because *you* are.

You can make a long stride forward by following simple and familiar rules. Moderate diet, moderate exercise, a reasonable amount of time and attention to grooming can work wonders. You don't need to pay a thousand dollars a week at a health spa. If you want a healthy, slimming diet you can live with, join a weight watchers class and follow their program. Try your nearest library for books on beauty care. Check out your favorite drugstore for the latest in cosmetics and beauty aids. Join an exercise class at the YWCA. Go bicycling or jogging for 20 minutes a day. If you use a car, park two blocks away from your destination instead of looking for the nearest parking space. A short walk will do you more good than fighting for the close parking spaces.

You know these things will work. If getting in shape is important enough to you, you'll do them. And you'll be doing them for yourself, not just your husband—which is exactly why they are likely to have the desired effect. Think about that.

I Don't See Why I Have To Do That!

If you're like most of us, you've been subjected to a horrendous list of books telling you how to become a better sexual performer. Any number of people out there seem to be warming up for the Sexual Olympics; once the starter's gun goes off, they start running as if they'd just been shot at.

Slow down.

Sex isn't a contest, and the attitude that a couple should win those Olympics every time they try amounts to a program for increasing marital dissatisfaction. Repeated failures lead to great pressure and stress, resulting in suspicion: "Why isn't she responding to me? Doesn't she love me?" "Why can't I fulfill myself sexually with him? Perhaps he's inexperienced and I need a better lover."

A "sexual response" does not mean that you undergo a fit or that your heart starts fibrillating every time you have intercourse. Some couples are so carried away by the *Joy of Sex* that they manage to take the joy out of sex. A sensual woman or man can find intercourse pleasant, enjoyable, interesting, cozy, or reassuring. You don't have to rate your sex life by the number of orgasms you had during the month or how often you were reduced to a quivering blob of speechless ecstasy!

The Hite Report, a survey of female sexuality, tells us about women who have "emotional orgasms." This, as you might guess, is a kind of orgasm that is not physical but, nevertheless, apparently very satisfactory. There are even "vicarious orgasms," in which a woman can have a fully satisfying emotional response at the moment her partner is having a biological one. What makes this "emotional orgasm" perfectly acceptable to the woman is the intensified sensation of closeness she and her man experience at such moments.

I'd like to tell you about an unmarried friend of mine, a classmate from college. The very model of a modern bluestocking, Laura didn't bother much about makeup, the way she dressed, or how she wore her hair. Her idea of a really romantic evening was to watch a poetry reading on public television. Her·ideal escort would have been a nice, serious, intelligent young man who shared her interests.

As you may have noticed, the supply of nice, serious, intelligent young men is so small they are practically an endangered species. Laura had to settle for dates with young men she didn't really like. And because she thought she *had* to enjoy sex, she really tried. Her efforts, instead of leading her to a sexual awakening, only awakened doubts about herself. She felt no tumultuous ecstasy, not even any primal yearning and burning. Such feelings, she had been told, were normal and natural, so she decided she must be abnormal and unnatural. Accepting this fact, she retired from the competitive struggle and withdrew her entry blank in the Sexual Olympics. She settled down to enjoy life without a man and became, as she told me one day candidly, "an unrepentant masturbator."

A year ago, Laura met a young man of the endangered species. They began seeing each other, and a sexual relationship developed naturally. Laura actually enjoyed making love. And I certainly enjoyed opening my mail recently and finding an invitation to their wedding!

Laura's "lack of sensuality" was caused by nothing more complicated than her not particularly liking the men she was forcing herself to go with.

I'm assuming that you like the man you're married to, or you wouldn't be reading this book. But you can still learn something important from Laura's story.

Women and men have emotional needs that have to be met. And a sensual response can happen only *after* those emotional needs have been met.

Clearly the Wives

According to reliable statistics, it is mostly women whose sexual needs are being slighted, overlooked, taken for granted. One study of a hundred middle-class couples, conducted by the University of Pittsburgh's Department of Psychiatry, revealed that almost half the women interviewed were having physical or psychological problems about sex. Only one-third of the men were. And only one man in seven even thought his wife had a problem with sex.

Obviously, the chief difficulty is one of communication. Without communication, the roots that nourish the vine of sensuality dry up. This same study identified some of the difficulties that women experience, including an inability to relax, lack of interest, too little foreplay, and too little tenderness.

"Among all the kinds of sexual problems, it is clearly the wives' 'sexual difficulties' that was the least well-tolerated," the study said. "Although it was once thought it was the man who wrote, produced and performed the sexual scenario, with the wife acting the role of 'extra,' at least within this better-educated, more affluent population the wife emerged as the major influence on the course of the drama. If the woman felt 'turned-off,' all sexual relations suffered as a result."

Clearly, this reluctance to speak up about sex is one of the deadlier enemies of a happy marriage. Women who won't try to communicate their needs in this area are, in many cases, acting out a childhood script in which they experienced rebuff or insufficient affection from their parents. They learned to ignore the pain of today's rejection and to hope tomorrow would be better. Needless to say, for such women, there is no tomorrow.

For most of us, merely trying to communicate will help enormously. "The journey of a thousand miles," says the Chinese proverb, "begins with a single step." Most journeys toward intimacy begin with the single step of trying to establish communication. Someone has to begin, or you will be like two people on opposite ends of an open telephone, each waiting for the other to speak first. Some women may object that it isn't in their nature to behave that way. What they mean is their repressions have been so well developed over the years that their natural instinct to express their needs has been stifled. Relax, and stop censoring the messages that your subconscious self wants to deliver. Above all, don't be ashamed of the fact that you have sexual needs. Everyone has. And that important first single step is to say what your needs are.

On the other side of the scale, however, is the woman who pours out her every indiscriminate thought and feeling. Retain some of your privacy. A hint of mystery maintains sexual appeal at a higher level. Don't empty everything out of the broom closet;

keep something in your treasure chest, a sense of something still to be disclosed. A woman can be intimate with a man without exposing to him every nerve and sinew, ligament, and bone. You're a woman, not the end result of an autopsy.

When you want to send your mate "revealing" messages, do so with a full awareness of your real motives. And then use delicacy and tact. You would have that much consideration for a stranger. Why show less for the person you love and with whom you have a deep emotional commitment?

These attitudes I've been talking about are only a few of the many that can prove deadly to a marriage. If you felt a quiver of recognition reading any of these, don't overlook it. Right now, that quiver may register only Point One on your emotional Richter Scale, but it is a portent of more dangerous quakes to come.

Put Yourself In His Shoes

Take a look at the growing number of second marriages. Men whose first wives found them impossible to live with are making other women happy. Their new wives consider them a blessing—however much their first wives thought them a curse.

Obviously, the difference is not so much in the men but in the women who married them.

Bill and I shared a beach cottage one summer with two friends, Lilly and Arthur. We liked them enormously and thought our summer at the beach would be fun. We were wrong, because Lilly and Arthur always seemed to be quarreling.

One day, Arthur was getting ready to drive to the station to catch a train. He was late. The train was scheduled to leave in only a few minutes. He called out impatiently, "Lilly, do you know where the car keys are?"

Lilly, white-faced with anger, appeared in the doorway. "I haven't touched your damn keys. I haven't even had the car. If anybody's lost them, it isn't me. It's you!"

A week later, Lilly was listening as Arthur was on the telephone making a golfing date with some pals. Before he could hang up, Lilly signaled him: "You haven't forgotten we're having dinner with the Wool-folks, have you?"

As soon as Arthur replaced the phone, he turned on her with cold fury. "What's the matter with you? Don't you think I'm capable of handling my own affairs? What makes you think I can't remember when I have a dinner date? How dare you interrupt me on the telephone with a stupid question like that? You were trying to make me look like a fool!"

Two incidents unrelated on the surface, but essentially alike. Both Lilly and Arthur were angry at what they interpreted as criticism. In both instances, no criticism was intended. Arthur was merely asking for Lilly's help to find his car keys, and Lilly only wanted reassurance that he was not making an arrangement that would conflict with previous plans.

How could they so misinterpret each other's meaning?

First of all, each had apparently been engaged in a verbal war of attrition for so long that they were supersensitized to *any* remark. Mutual resentments had built to the point that even the most innocent comment was construed as some kind of attack. One offense linked to another in an almost unbreakable chain of injury, resentment, counter offense, retaliation, and so on to infinity—or divorce.

Is there no way to stop the process short of such a tragic ending?

There is.

Put yourself in his shoes.

You may well ask, "Why can't he put himself in *my* shoes?" A perfectly reasonable question. But it's hard to make someone else do what *you* want. Why not try, for openers, giving yourself orders first. If you can't learn to do that, it's pure presumptuousness on your part to expect someone else to do what you can't!

Let's suppose, in that first instance, Lilly had not reacted so furiously to what she considered an accusation. Suppose, instead, she had just said, "I don't know where the keys are, but I'll try to help you find them."

A quarrel would have been avoided, certainly. More important, Arthur might not have been prompted to react so angrily when he felt himself challenged about a forgotten dinner date. Two big pluses, instead of two big minuses.

Seeds On Barren Ground

I'm sure you'd agree that this should be clear to anyone with even a modicum of intelligence. Yet day after day, in millions of households in this country and many millions more around the world, intelligent people are getting involved in precisely this kind of dispute. Why? Because the disputes don't involve intelligence—they are emotional. And emotional causes are often far removed indeed from what is being argued about.

If exactly the same situations (the missing car keys, the possibly conflicting dinner and golf dates) had confronted a couple who were habitually tender and loving with each other, there would have been no argument. But the seeds of love and tenderness don't flourish when tossed onto barren ground.

If Lilly had put herself in Arthur's shoes—if she could have made the effort to see herself as late on the way to the train, gathering together papers at the last minutes, and then suddenly noticing the car keys missing—she would not have reacted as she did. She would have tried to be helpful and would have sent Arthur off in a much better frame of mind, with memories of a loving wife instead of a bitter antagonist.

This would be true even if forgetfulness were one of Arthur's cardinal faults.

"Forgetfulness is one thing," I can hear a protesting reader respond. "That's the kind of fault it's easy to live with. Let's deal with some real faults, the kind that would tilt the halo of a saint!"

All right, then, let's consider the problem of Stephanie and Edward. Stephanie found Edward's fault a good deal harder to live with.

"He's a slob," she said flatly. "He doesn't deserve to live in a nice home. The way he behaves at home is a disgrace for the children to see. He'd sooner hang himself than his clothes. And he acts as though dumping his dirty underwear on the floor lends a decorative touch to the carpet. I have to keep after him all the time just so he'll be reasonably clean."

Stephanie didn't see any point in trying to put herself in Edward's shoes. "I probably couldn't find them anyway. He's dropped them anywhere in the house—anywhere he feels like taking them off!"

"Well, how are you trying to deal with the problem?" I asked her.

"By telling him I won't put up with it much longer if he doesn't change his ways. Since I'm his wife, I'm the only one who can point out what a slob he is. Somehow I've got to wake him up, make him see what a bad influence he is on his own children."

"You've been trying it that way. Is he getting any better?"

"Not a bit. But I'll keep after him until he does."

I persuaded Stephanie to try the experiment of putting herself in her husband's shoes. She did. After several sessions, she began to see that by constantly criticizing him, she was making him more defiant. He resented her constant harassment, her belittling him in front of the children.

Not long afterward, she made a breakthrough to a real emotional understanding. "He doesn't think he's bad because he's careless and sloppy and causes me inconvenience. This is just an easy, comfortable way for him to live. It's the way he *always* lived. He had an overindulgent mother who never asked him to do a thing around the house. He lived in a home with a maid. I think he'd behave differently if he thought it would make him happier, but he's too ticked off at me right now. He thinks I don't really accept him, and if the only way he can get me to accept him is by living up to the rules I set, he won't do it. He's too proud. As he sees it, I've been telling him that I value his neatness and the kind of example he sets in the home more than I do him. But that isn't so!"

Stephanie realized that the worsening sexual relations between them represented a hostile move on his part, a striking back to express resentment at the way she was treating him. The next step would have been open belligerence—and maybe divorce. But that isn't what Stephanie wanted.

Along with her clearer understanding of Edward's problem, Stephanie began to understand that her own compulsiveness about her home traced back, in part, to the fact that she had lived in a series of foster homes since she was 16. This was the first home she had of her own, and naturally she wanted it to be spotless.

She held a family conference and asked the children which of the objectionable chores they would undertake in the interests of family harmony. She got more cooperation than she expected. Their teenage son and daughter were so anxious to see an end to the ceaseless squabbling at home that they'd have agreed to do anything!

The objectionable chores were put on a revolving list, so that neither Stephanie nor the kids had to do them regularly. It was an orderly system. After a while, Edward began to pitch in a little himself.

"I really think he was so grateful and relieved that

I wasn't constantly hassling him, he tried the same process himself," Stephanie said. "He put himself in my shoes!"

There is a coda to the story. The week before Christmas last year, Stephanie and Edward went out to a party. When they got home, there was a huge Christmas tree set up in the living room. And their daughter and son, standing beside it, shouted, "Merry Christmas!"

"It was the first time in my life I had a real Christmas tree," Stephanie said. "Edward had bought it and stored it in the basement, and our children put it up while we were at the party. It was such a surprise that all I could do was sit in a chair and say through my tears, 'I love you. I love you all.' That tree made me know for the first time that I was in my own home—a real home all my own. Ed and I drank champagne and that night we slept wrapped in each other's arms!"

A New Understanding

You may find that a little thought and effort makes it easy for you to put yourself in your husband's shoes. If not, here are some steps that will definitely help:

1. Choose a quiet moment in which you are alone. Sit down in a comfortable chair—don't lie down, or you may drift off to sleep. The purpose is relaxation, not a catnap.
2. Close your eyes, and take a long slow breath and

hold it. Exhale slowly. Repeat until you feel so relaxed you're almost boneless.

3. Make a deliberate effort to clear your mind of all thought. Picture your mind as a blackboard, and the moment an unwanted thought appears wipe it off.

4. Now: Try to recall the last time you had an argument with your husband. Take an incident that really disturbed you, in which he was being particularly arbitrary or unreasonable.

5. Put yourself back in that situation. Picture it with absolute clarity. See the expression on his face, hear the words both of you said.

6. Trace through the entire incident from beginning to end. Envision the setting, the action, the gestures, until you have everything as perfectly fixed in memory as can be.

7. Now, draw yourself up above the scene in space, looking down at it. See yourself as a spectator would see you and your husband.

8. Descend again quickly, but not into your own skin. Into his. Now you must see through his eyes. Again, picture the setting, the action, the gestures. Then look at yourself through *his* eyes.

9. When you see as he sees, the next step is to listen to your voice as he hears it.

10. Run through the incident again, remembering all the same words, and actions, *but from inside his skin*. Experience his emotions—anger, fear, boredom, impatience, whatever—exactly as he is feeling them.

This system works. When you do it faithfully, you will gain a new understanding of your husband, a new acceptance and sympathy for him. And this is a sure route to increasing sensual feeling.

Then What Happened?

"Last night Norman was packing his clothes, intending to leave me and our two small children," Beth told me. She is a tall, rangy, 34-year-old woman, who dresses in a style that used to be called sloppy and is now known as casual. She wore a man's shirt with the tails hanging out over patched jeans, and her bare feet were in moccasins. "I know the bastard wants out. He's been itching to get away from me and the kids and responsibilities. I had to beg him not to go, to give me a little more time. But I know it's going to happen soon, and the strain is driving me crazy. I'm so hurt that about ten times a day I go into the bathroom and have a good cry.

"I guess it's hopeless. Maybe it'd be better if he just went ahead and left now. I'll have to make a fresh start sometime."

I've only known Beth about a year, but she obviously needed someone to confide in. When I asked why she thought Norman wanted to leave, she couldn't think of a specific reason. So I told her to try the method of putting herself in his shoes. She was skeptical but willing to make the attempt.

At our next meeting, Beth had obviously made

progress. "Maybe it's me," she said. "I'm not as young or pretty as when we got married a dozen years ago. But Norman never seemed to care. One of the things that attracted me in the first place was that he wasn't one of those shallow types who only seemed to be interested in the size of my bosom or my behind. He didn't give me the uneasy feeling that on our first date he was trying to figure out how soon he could get me into bed. He was sensitive and idealistic. It was absolutely fabulous to be wanted by a man like that."

Then she spoke what were, for her, the key words: "I'll have to pull myself together, do something about how I look. Nobody would want me the way I am now."

"Doesn't Mommy Look Pretty Tonight?"

Beth and I didn't see each other again for several weeks. Bill and I had gone to California on a special project. When I returned I called her, half expecting to hear that she and Norman had split up. To my surprise, she sounded bright and cheerful, and invited me to lunch with her the next day.

"You were the first one to clue me in on what the trouble might be," she told me at lunch. "By the way, how do I look?"

She looked different, all right. Gone were the man's shirt and the patched jeans. She was wearing a sexy, adorable wrap dress. The Beth I knew hardly ever wore makeup or lipstick, because she had the kind of clear tanned complexion that can go without makeup. Now she looked like a million dollars with bright lipstick and glowing color on her cheeks, and I think she even had on eyelashes.

"You look terrific," I told her. "If this is what I clued you into, I'm glad!"

"This is just part of it. After I tried that method of putting myself in his shoes, I realized how stupid and unfair it was to expect Norman to want me, if nobody else could, just because he was my husband. I didn't really want to attract other men. I wanted to attract *him*. I wanted him to love me again the way he did when we were first married. He used to tell me I was the loveliest creature in the world, that he was 'infatuated' with my body.

"I made up my mind to try my darndest to make him feel that way about me again! My breakfast costume was usually an old bathrobe and slippers, and I never bothered with makeup. One morning I got up earlier, showered, sprayed on cologne, and put moisturizer on my face. By the time Norman showed up for breakfast, I'd gotten into a pretty daytime dress. It was trouble, but when I saw how he looked at me, it was worth every minute of the trouble!"

That day, she went to a hairdresser who got her messy hair into shape. When Norman returned home that night, Beth was wearing a "going out" dress and she'd put on stockings and high heels. Norman asked where they were going. She said nowhere, that she had just dressed up for him. He then volunteered to take her somewhere "just to show you off," but she persuaded him that she'd rather stay home and have dinner alone together. "Doesn't Mommy look pretty tonight?" their four-year-old daughter asked at bedtime. "I wouldn't be surprised if you've got the prettiest Mommy in the world," Norman answered.

That night, she and Norman rediscovered what had gone out of their marriage. They found a prescription that banished tiredness and tension, and put back the sparkle and zest. Like so many "middle-aging" couples, they had simply bored themselves into sexual inactivity. They had been unpacking their lives—and when that happens, too often someone, either the husband or the wife, starts packing to go.

Fortunately, Beth found out what her problem was in time.

Elaine and Herb were in a different situation. Whatever she wanted, he seemed to want—or so he let her believe. But somehow their marriage was on a downhill course.

"I don't even like him any more," Elaine told me. "He's a big, spoiled, lazy kid."

Both Elaine and Herb were disappointed with their marriage, yet too fearful to even discuss it. Each hung back, waiting for the other to break the stalemate, and meanwhile their growing discontent—never expressed—was causing them more and more unhappiness.

Finally, they sat down to discuss their problem. Elaine drew Herb out to discover how things looked from his point of view. One of his biggest gripes was their house. Elaine simply couldn't understand that. The house was spacious with lovely grounds. She had for several summers been planting flowers among some granite boulders on their back lawn, and now her "rock garden" was the talk of the neighborhood. She was sure the real explanation lay elsewhere. She tried to explain their failing marriage in sexual terms, for she had read often enough that a sexual problem was usually behind most marital problems.

Then she took my advice, and tried putting herself in her husband's shoes. "Almost at once I realized what he meant. The house was too expensive, he had to struggle to meet the mortgage payments, and it was too far from his work. The pressures of work plus commuting, hassling with buses and trains, made him so exhausted that it was affecting his sex drive. And I'd thought this was just another symptom of our failing marriage!"

She talked the situation over with Herb, and they decided to sell their house and move into a condominium much nearer to Herb's work. That solved the problem of commuting, and therefore Herb's weariness at night. The sexual problem that had seemed so crucial simply vanished—along with the real cause of it!

There are literally millions of unhappy couples who don't make an attempt to see the world from each other's point of view. Marriage is a union of two

different people who continually must make adjustments in order to maintain an affectionate relationship.
Everyone will agree with that statement in theory, but
how many really act as if they believe it? How many are
willing to put themselves into the other person's shoes?

The High Cost of Loving

Two Christmases ago Bill and I attended the wedding of beautiful 20-year-old Esther-Jean, the daughter of a close friend. Eight months later, she and her husband Adam had decided to go through a trial separation.

"It seemed like we were bickering and arguing about money all the time," Esther-Jean told me. "Adam was generous when it came to spending on himself, for his hobbies or going on vacations—his kind of vacations. He just couldn't see spending money for things I wanted, like clothes and extra luxuries for myself, or pretty things for the house. When the department store bills came in, he'd hit the ceiling. I wasn't used to that because when I was living at home, my parents took care of my charge accounts. When I signed up for a dance-exercise class, Adam even criticized me for that.

I pointed out that we spent a lot more for his camping equipment and fishing tackle than we did for my classes. It led to a lot of bickering."

On the other hand, this was Adam's story: "From the beginning, I had to handle finances or we'd have been in real trouble. Esther-Jean just wasn't very smart about money. We had a joint account, but she used it for whatever she wanted. Whenever I complained about some expense, her face darkened. She expected me to back down, I suppose, like her family always did when she got in one of her moods. But I wouldn't. I couldn't let her have her way when she's so incredibly bad at handling money."

Esther-Jean had begun to "punish" Adam for what she considered his stinginess by withholding sex. As Adam put it, "Whenever I was in a loving mood, she acted like a block of wood." The two of them had become trapped in a vicious circle—arguing about money, arguing about sex.

Fortunately, the parents of both Esther-Jean and Adam got them together to resolve the problem. As a result of that family conference, Adam agreed that there should be a clear division between "his money" and "Esther-Jean's money." Neither should have to account to the other for what they spent. They also set up a category which they called "our money," to pay the rent, grocery, and electricity bills, insurance, etc. This was a big concession for Adam because he didn't want separate checking accounts, believing that the method worked against "togetherness" in marriage. But he accepted that Esther-Jean needed some personal money to do with what she liked. For her part, Esther-Jean conceded that she would have to mend her extravagant ways and live within her reduced means.

Both Esther-Jean and Adam are trying hard to make the new arrangement work. At least they both are now aware of the close interconnection between dollars-and-cents and sensuality, and Esther-Jean admits she was wrong to use sex as a method of "punishment."

Less Than Total Commitment

The emotional framework of marriage is often as complex and fragile as a spider's web. Money can be a serious threat. Muriel and Sol, for example, were partners in a real estate investment firm for several years before they decided to get married. Muriel wanted to draw up a contract providing for the disposal of the property in the event of a divorce.

Sol objected. He felt that if they committed themselves to a marriage, it must mean they trusted each other.

He says, "I guess I felt insecure because Muriel wanted the same kind of legal protection after we were married that we'd had when we were business partners. It's as if she were announcing, 'No marriage can last forever, but a business arrangement will.' As far as I was concerned, her attitude was destructive. It was threatening. Why go into something like a marriage with the idea that it won't work out?"

Muriel admitted, "I'm very insecure about money, because when my father left my mother he took everything. We were very poor for a long time, and it made me anxious about such a thing happening to me. I'd be repeating my mother's mistake if I didn't make sure that what was mine was in my name, so nobody could take it away from me."

Sol hadn't realized how deep her feelings were on the subject. "I'm a little more wary now. There's something less than total commitment between us. I don't think either of us are quite as secure."

The importance of freeing the emotional side of marriage from the financial side is aptly, if sadly, illustrated by both these true stories. Over a period of time, the prognosis is poor for a married couple that allows money to become a divisive factor in how they relate to each other. When distrust or dissension develops in monetary matters, the possibilities for emotional trust and sharing are correspondingly reduced. Even if you can't completely subtract your financial problems from the emotional area of marriage, you can work at making them less intrusive. A good rule to remember is that numbers have no emotions; arithmetic is a science devoid of feeling and should be treated as such. Two and two may always make four, but they don't necessarily add up to happiness in marriage.

Coping With Secret Worries

My friend Terry, an unusually beautiful woman of 34, noticed a waning of her husband Don's sexual interest. Don was in good, sound health, was not running around with other women or drinking heavily, so she saw no reason why sex should have become a problem.

She was wise enough to know that nagging Don was not the solution. She was also patient and willing to wait until his desire returned, convinced that the condition was temporary and that the underlying cause would surface if given the opportunity to do so.

One evening, Don came home in a really bad temper. He was having a problem with an associate who was unwilling to carry his full share of work. Don was filling in for the other man in addition to doing his job. The boss did not seem aware of what was going on. He even seemed to favor the other man, who was more of a socializer than Don.

Don remained tense all through dinner. There were clear intimations of an argument to come. Sure enough, that evening the storm broke. Going through their checkbook, Don found that Terry had bought clothes for the children at a local store. He demanded to know why she thought the children needed new clothes "at a time like this," why she couldn't have waited to shop in a large department store noted for its cheaper prices.

Terry said he was being unfair. She didn't over-indulge the children, and spent less money on them than the wives she knew whose husbands earned less than Don. She accused him of being stingy, not caring about his own children. Don exploded and marched out of the house.

During the long hours in which Terry waited for his return—not being sure when or if he would return—she had time to reassess her position. His concern about spending might be connected with his work at the office. If so, she should have offered him her support rather than a display of temper.

When Don did come home, a little tipsy, at one o'clock in the morning, Terry didn't reproach him. Instead, she said, "I know what a bad time you're having. I'm really sorry, and I'll make it up to you—if I can."

Her attitude released pressures that had been building up in him. He began talking, his words tumbling over each other. It turned out he was afraid of losing his job because the boss liked his lazy associate better. At his age, he felt it wouldn't be easy to find a job that paid as well. He and Terry had almost no savings, and he worried that he wouldn't be able to support her in the style she'd become accustomed to. Without the prestige and security of a good-paying job, he was afraid he would be unable to hold her. He had been trying to cope with his secret worries, alone, for months.

They sat up most of the night talking. Don was so exhilarated by talking out his problems that he felt no need of sleep. And Terry was so pleased by the renewed warmth between them that she had no desire to sleep either. At six o'clock in the morning they finally went to the bedroom, where they made love for the first time in a month.

At breakfast, Don was in a much more optimistic mood. He announced, "I'm going to my boss today and find out where I stand. I may even ask him for a raise. If I'm doing two men's work I might as well get paid for it."

P.S. He got his raise. The boss was fully aware of how much extra work Don was doing, and was also aware of the other man's shortcomings. If anyone was going to be fired, the boss told him, it would not be Don but his rival!

Much can be learned by listening for what your husband is really telling you. In fact, alert, sympathetic listening is one of the true hallmarks of the happily married. Anyone can listen with the ears; the trick is to listen with the heart, for we understand more in our hearts than words can tell us.

Mike Douglas, the well-known talk-show host, tells about the first years of his marriage, when he and his wife Gen were teenagers. Gen was 18 when their twins were born, and Mike was only 19. He sang with a band and traveled around the country on small jobs. The Douglases had to be separated a great deal because Mike felt he couldn't afford to take his family along.

Things reached such a critical point that Gen was crying herself to sleep every night. She didn't want to be married to a man in show business; she decided that perhaps she didn't really love Mike as much as she'd thought she did. Mike sat her down to talk it over. They discovered that she was having a difficult time because she was so lonely. Gen was unhappy not because she didn't love her husband, but because she did.

Mike got the message and reached a decision. Wherever he went, and at whatever cost, he would take his family. "I can't tell you how often we were together in a single hotel room, filled with babies, bottles, and diapers. But I'm certain that the effort we made to stay together is the main reason our marriage has lasted."

Mike and Gen are full partners in business—he never makes a move without consulting her, and he credits her with most of his present success. Their marriage has not only lasted, Mike and Gen are among the very few real honeymooners for life in show business. All because they put their marriage ahead of money and had the courage and intelligence to confront their problems—to establish the kind of communication that led to the right decision. Mike was wise enough to put their emotional needs first. Today, Mike and Gen's only financial problem is how to spend all the money they make!

The Future May Never Come

It's a much different story with Heather and Lou. She works as an indexer for a woman's magazine, and

Lou is an editorial researcher. Their combined income barely covers the expense of their family. They have three children, ages 14, 11, and 8. Lou's work is on assignment, and there are often long stretches when he is at home. When Heather was away at the magazine's office, Lou pitched in and helped with housework.

For a while, they were having serious problems. Lou resented it when Heather complained that the oven didn't get cleaned. After he'd washed and waxed the kitchen floor, he'd be furious if the children came in and made it dirty again. If Heather defended them, explaining they were "just acting like kids," Lou would get livid with rage.

Finally, feeling that "Lou's nose was definitely out of joint," Heather convinced him they should visit a marriage counselor. To her surprise, "the counselor seemed to feel *I* was the one at fault. The trouble was that I'd submerged Lou too much in the family, so that he no longer had a distinct masculine image. Relegating household chores to him had made him feel like a failure, a kitchen drudge instead of a man. He didn't even believe his children had any respect for him.

"Because I was good at details, I'd taken over most of the financial chores—keeping records for income tax, balancing the checkbook, paying the children their weekly allowance. I appeared to be the money-earner. If the children asked why we didn't have enough money, I would explain that I was doing everything I could and they mustn't expect too much from me. From *me!* As if my income would come anywhere near buying all the things we needed. It wouldn't even have bought the necessities. But somehow I never stressed that fact!"

Naturally, Lou rebelled. He wouldn't walk out on Heather or his family, and he wasn't the kind of man who'd stand up and fight. So he settled for avoiding sexual relations. As the counselor explained it to Heather, Lou was telling her, "You've made me less a man, so I'll perform that way. See how you like it."

"I was a fool," Heather says. "The marriage counselor opened my eyes. Lou and I hadn't had a vacation in years—what money we saved was for the family, a fund so our oldest son would go to college, life insurance and Blue Cross, things like that. We were living our whole lives for a future that might never come. It occurred to us we ought to have some fun ourselves, while we were still healthy enough to enjoy it."

Heather and Lou reviewed their budget with an eye for present pleasures. They decided it didn't matter too much if they never got a new living room rug or if their daughter's bedroom needed a new chest of drawers. The children took the news well when Heather informed them that she and Lou were going to Bermuda for ten days and her sister was coming to the house to stay with them.

"That vacation saved our marriage," Heather says. "I'm convinced of it. Oh, we would never have gotten divorced or anything like that, but everything would have kept going downhill. Finally, we wouldn't have had a marriage—just a working arrangement. In the hotel in St. George, we found out why we fell in love with each other in the first place. Falling in love again was almost as easy as falling into bed!"

A Tantalizing Towel

No matter how tight finances are, there is always some way to keep them from negatively affecting the sensual content of your marriage. You set aside money every week for the sober, responsible things of your lives. How about the frivolous joys that once were part of your courtship? You were just as poor, or poorer, when you were "going together," but you always could go to a movie or a dance, buy an ice cream soda or an unexpected, hence delightful, little gift. Difficult as it was, somehow you were always able to come up with enough money. Now that you're making more, you seem to have less to spend on such pleasures.

The truth is, you don't have less to spend, you've just put that kind of pleasure far down on your list of priorities. Money goes for rent, utilities, insurance, the children's clothes, medical bills—never for what might keep your marriage a honeymoon.

Jacqueline and Shawn are a young couple with two kids and absolutely no money. Yet they have more fun together than almost anyone. They've been married ten years, but are obviously so much in love I have no hesitation in listing them as honeymooners for life.

The High Cost Of Loving

Jacqueline is a very sensuous young female. She has a nice body, nothing extraordinary, but she makes it speak in every known human language, including Sanskrit. She communicates sex appeal with a capital S without having to strut or swing her hips. Even when she lifts a tray to bring it to the dinner table, you are suddenly aware of how attractive her bosom is because her shoulders have that subtle back-and-forth movement. When she walks across a room, it's clear that here's a woman who enjoys having a body and knows just what to do with it.

I asked her if she had any tips for this chapter. She laughed, then replied seriously, "It's easy for some women to be attractive to men. They spend so much money on facials and hairdressers, manicures and expensive perfumes, the kind of clothes that could make almost any woman's figure look spectacular.

"But I decided a long time ago that sensuality is mostly mind over matter. It doesn't cost anything to come out of a bath wearing a skimpy towel. Let your husband have a tantalizing look. Shawn didn't notice that most of the time when I come out that way, I wear high-heeled slippers so I won't have a flat-footed look. That's unflattering to almost any woman's legs. Shawn has often mentioned that I turn him on just by the way I brush my hair or put on makeup. I think women should practice doing these things—with some regard for how they'll look to their husbands. A woman should seem relaxed and graceful, at ease inside her body. If she's comfortable, men will be comfortable around her. None of this costs a penny, because no artificial aids are needed.

"But the biggest reason Shawn and I still feel 'that way' about each other is that we try to make our budget work for us, not against us."

"How do you do that?" I asked her.

"Before we put aside any money for necessities, we put what we can afford into our Love Jar. You'd be surprised how quickly it mounts up. We use the money to buy anything that looks like it might be exciting, or fun, or help us maintain that old feeling. Sometimes it's a magazine with an article that sounds particularly promising—suggesting new ways we can become more intimate and loving. Another time it's a black G-string that Shawn saw advertised and thought I'd be irresistible in. Sometimes it's for something that seems to have no connection with how we are sexually with each other—but turns out to be. For example, we saved up enough to spend two days at a dude ranch. And we still talk about those two days. It's our favorite way of turning on. We were away from the children, feeling free. We responded to each other and really let our feelings go. We even made love riding astride—on horseback!"

What Jacqueline and Shawn learned is to put the right priority on their spending. No matter how tight your budget, there is always room for what I call "indiscretionary" spending. And that will invariably turn out to be the best money you ever spent, because, in effect, you're investing in your own marriage.

Checks and Daisies

There are many little ways in which you can heighten the sensual content of marriage at no risk of unbalancing your budget. Since you give presents of some kind for birthdays, anniversaries, Christmas, etc., how about a little remembrance of a particularly lovely night? One couple I interviewed give each other a silver spoon (for spooning?) engraved with the date they want to record for history. They have quite a collection.

Don't make the mistake that Burt made, though. Burt long ago got into the habit of paying cash. He sends checks to all his relatives for birthdays and Christmas. "Let 'em buy what *they* want," he says, but it's really to save himself the trouble of choosing an appropriate gift—and everyone knows it and measures their gratitude accordingly. Burt thinks money can buy anything.

He carries the same attitude over into his marriage. When his wife Ruth has a birthday, he gives her an expensive present—picked out by his secretary. On one occasion he even forgot what it was his secretary had gotten. On still another occasion, he neglected to sign the card that his secretary carefully attached to the gift box. Burt is the kind of husband who is willing to spend, but unwilling to put any thought into it—and that kind of gift-giving gives a woman no real emotional satisfaction.

The crowning proof of Burt's insensitivity may be hard to believe, but Ruth assures me it is true. Whenever they have sex, Burt slips a check under her pillow. It's a generous check, but she says, "It makes me feel like a whore." Perhaps not surprisingly, Ruth recently began an affair with a young actor. If her lover sends her daisies, she is more thrilled by the bouquet than by her husband's most generous checks.

Small wonder. Any gift which carries a message of real feeling is far more valuable than one that does not. A corporation may send you a bonus at the end of the year and you may be glad to have the money—but you know perfectly well that it's an impersonal gesture. "Who steals my purse, steals trash," Shakespeare said. Any gift that's from a purse, not a person, is essentially trashy. You can be grateful for the money, but you can't be grateful for the thought.

I'll cite a different instance. Holly is married to a hard-driving, self-sufficient business executive. Philip is not as crass as Burt, but he *is* preoccupied. To him, exchanging gifts just represents so much time wasted from his busy day. Recently, on their fifteenth wedding anniversary, Holly wrote him a little poem about how much she liked to lie beside him in bed. Philip, the hardboiled executive who would not have batted an eye if she'd bought him a new Rolls Royce, was in tears when he read it. He has the poem encased in plastic and always carries it in his wallet.

Sex and Math

When financial problems become a threat to marital happiness, here are a few tips to help you avoid useless friction.

Don't have sex at a time when you're in the middle of a financial argument or when money problems are particularly acute. A woman who chooses a tense and difficult time in which to make love is simply bucking the odds. When you are going over bills and writing checks, when bank balances are dwindling and expenditures being reviewed, there are bound to be feelings of resentment. If your husband criticizes your spending, you'll be annoyed. If you can't reconcile the bank balance or remember why there's a missing check in the checkbook, he'll be exasperated. When he adds up the food bill for the month, he'll think you're a Russian saboteur. Secretly, most men believe the whole problem of inflation could be solved if women would just stop spending so much in the supermarkets. In turn, women think men would have a much better grasp on the reality of inflation if they had to work the supermarket shift.

That kind of disagreement does not foster intimacy in the bedroom. There's no *physical* reason why you can't make love at such times, but the emotional set-up is wrong. Sex is a marvelous way for easing tensions, but not the kind induced at bill-paying or income tax time. If you hated math in school and still think that

Isosceles is a Greek philosopher, your husband isn't likely to be in a sensual mood at bedtime after an evening spent warring with the checkbook.

Kiss and Splurge

You *can* turn the weekly or monthly budget survey into a pleasant occasion, but you will need a little cooperation from the inscrutable gods who look after family finances. For example, if the bank balance happens to jibe to the last decimal point with the bank's, what better way to celebrate than by making love? If you and your husband make it a practice to reward yourself this way, you may even learn to be more careful with addition and subtraction.

If there's any area in which things have improved this month over last, make a point of it. Suppose you spent less on groceries, or you've cut the electric bill or the telephone bill, or you've gotten an unexpected refund or rebate, or the department store bill includes that item you took back for credit so it really *isn't* as high as it seems—point with pride, kiss each other, and splurge.

Yes, *splurge*. This is money you *might* have spent on some less rewarding purpose, so it's practically free. It's like finding a betting chip on the floor in a Las Vegas gambling casino. Push your luck. Go out to dinner and order a bottle of wine, or buy tickets to a movie or a play or a concert. Do whatever you can to set up a celebratory and romantic mood.

Appreciate, Appreciate!

Never, *never* take any gift from your husband for granted. Remember: sensuality and sentiment are never far removed from each other. Which is why you'd be wise to show appreciation for *anything* that is offered out of love. No matter what it costs.

Julie's husband Miles bought her a black jade bracelet for Christmas. A thoughtful gift, because Julie does love jade and had a nice small collection. Unfortunately, she also had a more expensive black jade bracelet that she wore often.

When Miles saw her expression on opening his present, his spirits sank. He suddenly remembered the other bracelet and apologized, saying the fact had simply slipped his mind. Julie's only comment, "That's just like you, dear," led to the bitterest feud of their marriage.

No matter how much she may have wished that Miles was more observant, she should have been more understanding. Husbands often don't have a memory for such things, important as they are to women. Whatever the cost, the gift was given out of love. When Julie rejected it, she was asking for the trouble she got.

Appreciation is an excellent preventive medicine for many of the ailments that affect a marriage. And no one gets to be a honeymooner for life who doesn't learn the art of appreciation.

Come Out Fighting— End Up Loving

Your husband arrives fully equipped with his own needs, interests, opinions, biases, and demands. Where the edges of your differing personalities meet and grind against each other, there is bound to be friction.

Friction causes a spark of anger, and the spark can ignite a quarrel.

And, believe it or not, that's fine.

Quarreling can be an effective way for married couples to discharge the inevitable tensions that arise from two people trying to live with each other. There may be a couple somewhere who lives in absolute peace and harmony, who likes to do exactly the same things, who agrees entirely about religion, politics, taste, tradition, custom, in-laws, and how to raise children. If there is such a couple, they're probably clones. And they'll bore each other to death.

I know, and I'm sure you do, couples who claim to exist in perfect harmony. In many instances, they are holding back any resentments, fears, anxieties, and hopes in order to preserve the shallow appearance of total agreement. But they are not communicating on a serious level. These are the so-called "perfect marriages" that blow to smithereens and leave everyone asking, "Why? They were so happy!"

Nothing is more dangerous than suppressing emotion. You might as well try to cover a hand grenade with a scarf.

David's Rival

A young artistic couple, Rae and David—she's a talented painter and he's a concert pianist—provide a striking example of how not to deal with latently destructive emotions. For the first few years of their marriage, David was the provider. He was in demand as a pianist, both in individual concerts and with symphony orchestras. Rae was in charge of the family. She was the cook and the nanny for their difficult six-year-old boy. She had too little time to pursue her own career as a painter. Instead of demanding more consideration for her talent—hiring household help or asking David to accept more family responsibility—she shouldered her burdens without complaint.

Surprisingly, her career took wing. She sold several paintings, then had a one-woman exhibition that was a smashing commercial success and got rave critical reviews. For the first time, Rae felt financially secure. She hired a woman to clean house, cook meals, and take some of the care of her young son off her shoulders. She rented a studio to work in so she wouldn't be interrupted by other tasks.

"David would come to the studio," she says, "and look over my shoulder while I was working. He'd make derogatory comments while I seethed. David is a gifted musician, but his opinion on painting isn't worth anything. Yet he expected me to defer to him. Finally I blew up. I told him I didn't want him to come to the studio ever again, that my painting was more important to me than he was. He became furious. Everything escalated from there. Now we're living apart. I'm not happy and neither is he, but neither of us is going to give in. Maybe artists aren't meant to be married because they're already married to their art."

But there are thousands of married artists who have managed to mesh their career needs with their marriage needs. Like most unhappy people, Rae is trying to convince herself that there is no such thing as happiness.

When she first began to feel that her career was being neglected, she should not have let her resentments go unspoken. She and David might have resolved the conflict then, before it became serious. Instead, the problem continued to build. David saw her career as a rival. But he didn't try to express his feeling honestly—it came out only as an attack on her work. When, at last, David was faced with her real needs and aspirations, he no longer had the flexibility to cope. They had drifted apart emotionally, and the gap between had become too great to bridge.

You're Not A Geyser

Intimate relationships, by their very nature, generate conflict. These conflicts must be worked out as they arise. One method of working out conflict is by argument.

I'm not advocating the kind of argument that raises barriers between people. Nor am I saying hooray for quarrels and let the cutlery fly! That kind of argument doesn't clear the air. It pollutes it.

When a woman screams at her husband that his untidy habits are driving her crazy, she creates hostility and tension. Calling someone a "pig" or "stupid" or a "bum" may help to relieve your angry feelings, but it's guaranteed to evoke the sort of response that will heat up the emotional atmosphere.

A good way to avoid this kind of counter-productive arguing is to restrict your point of view to a narrow base. If your husband falls asleep watching TV when you are anxious to discuss something, you don't have to let this single episode open a whole Pandora's box of pent-up hostility. You don't have to begin a tirade about how cold and inconsiderate and unloving he is. Isolate the incident that has just caused your annoyance. Why did he have to watch TV at that particular moment, for example? An argument of that size is much easier to handle than a whole war about your conflicting needs.

Another constructive measure is to try to analyze exactly *why* you're angry. Were you snapping at your husband even though he hadn't done anything to make you so angry? You might be making life miserable for yourself and him for an entirely different reason than you think. We all have frustrations that make us feel anxious and depressed, and these sometimes erupt in unexpected ways.

One woman told me that she had picked a terrible fight with her husband on the eve of a long-awaited vacation. "It started with the way he was packing the luggage. I became furious. When I calmed down I asked myself why I had done it, and discovered I wasn't looking forward to the vacation at all. We were going to a lakeside resort where there was a good deal of sailing. My husband loves to sail, but I don't. I didn't expect to get any pleasure from a vacation like that, and the effort of getting ready for it seemed more trouble than it was worth. I couldn't change my feeling about that, but knowing my real reason did help ease the problem somewhat. We went to the resort as planned, and he did spend a lot of his time sailing. But I spent a lot of my time lolling under a beach umbrella and reading novels."

Stress causes arguments, just as it causes physical symptoms like headaches, backaches, and indigestion. When you're under stress you're ready to do battle at any provocation. You react to things differently. You may find it harder to concentrate or to focus your thoughts. Your blood pressure shoots up, you rage and scream. You may even think, I can't stand this kind of pressure any more. If you do, take heed. Your subconscious is giving you a warning. You may indeed not be able to stand it any more—and your husband also may not be able to stand being a victim of your stress.

One of the most crucial tasks in making a marriage succeed is to use anger constructively. That doesn't mean blowing off steam for its own sake—you're not a geyser, you're a human being. You have the intelligence to seek out the reason for your anger and to do something about it.

A feeling that is hidden doesn't go away. It retreats into your subconscious. Imperceptibly, affection cools a little and you're not as open and trusting. Every hurt that's unexpressed, every annoyance that's stifled, detracts from the sensual ambiance in which marriage thrives.

He Went Berserk

Florrie and Will are a good example of the dreadful consequences of the wrong kind of arguing. Florrie was disappointed in Will because, after 12 years of marriage, he was not a moneymaker. Florrie was earning more money than Will and never let him forget it. Whenever they went on vacation, she reminded him that her money was paying for it. This led to more arguments in which Florrie returned to her favorite theme: he was not a good provider. She was a scold, forever criticizing, nagging, lecturing, reproaching, reproving, and reprimanding. When scolding wasn't enough, she resorted to tears.

At other times Florrie adopted a maternal attitude. Or she employed the Fire-and-Ice treatment, becoming furious at Will for not being better than he was and then putting him into the deep freeze of her disfavor and not speaking to him. She also used the Coax-and-Cajole ploy, in which she tried to sweet-talk him into doing what she wanted. Not surprisingly, her efforts had about the same impact as trying to sweet-talk Mount Rushmore.

The basic problem was that Florrie was treating her husband not as a man but as a child. The Coax-and-Cajole approach works fine when you're trying to induce an infant to take one more spoonful of oatmeal, but it isn't that effective when you're trying to get a 41-year-old man to change his ways.

What happened in this marriage? Will became virtually impotent. As he says, "Something happened to me. I couldn't perform. My body felt numb, almost paralyzed. Florrie was pretty upset. She probably didn't mean to, but the fact remains that when she kept putting me down this happened."

Furious at his own sexual inadequacy and helplessness, Will exploded when Florrie told him that if he couldn't function in bed, he really *was* good for nothing. One night he went berserk and tried to strangle her. He was temporarily out of his mind, but fortunately one of the children overheard her screams and stopped him. Will was so ashamed he left home and has not returned—not even to get his clothes.

Silence As Argument

Florrie and Will's story offers an extreme example of how the wrong kind of arguing can make hostility worse rather than provide a safety valve. On the other hand, if a hostile impulse is faced with honesty and discussed rationally and openly, a wife and husband can forge a strong bond of empathy. People who really love each other don't like to stay angry. Underneath, they each know they're not 100 percent right. What they want is a chance to get across their point of view. Then they are willing to make compromises. The argument itself drains off dangerous emotions that might otherwise accumulate.

Those who are able to give vent to their feelings avoid the prolonged "silences" that are really a form of argument without words. And when the anger cools, they have the wonderful joy of making up.

Taking Anger To Bed

"What I think is most important about our arguments with each other is when we make up," says Caroline, a happily married woman of 28 years. "We're able to laugh about it later. If you can't quarrel and make up with your husband, the chances are pretty good that you can't be happy with him."

"After having been married for 17 years, I can tell you plenty about arguments," says Deborah. "I quarrel with him about almost anything—the fact that he TV channel-hops without asking what I want to see, or that he doesn't pick up his dirty socks and throw them in the hamper, or he leaves a ring in the bathtub, or that he calls me from California when there's a freezing snowstorm here in New Jersey and asks, 'How's the weather where you are?' He has the same kind of annoyances with me. But our spats don't last long, and when they're over we always know better where we stand."

A dispute can help to give a wife and husband a better perspective, enabling each of them to see the other's problem more clearly. Even a sharp exchange of viewpoints helps you arrive at a better solution for what's bothering you. Such a relationship is less fragile than that of a wife and husband who pretend not to disagree, basically because they are afraid that their marriage cannot stand the strain. A couple who argues constructively is more likely to grow sensually close. They'll gain deeper insight into each other, and they won't suffer from the guilt of harboring ugly emotions. Nor will their sex lives be affected by their taking hidden anger to bed with them.

Sex is often used as a concealed form of argument. We all know the ploy of withholding sex as a way of expressing anger. The wife's complaint of being "tired" or "having a headache," the husband's "lack of interest," frequently conceals animosity. If employed by the wife, most husbands resent this tactic more than any other, even if they don't make an issue of it. The next time they may try (perhaps subconsciously) to spoil sex by ejaculating too quickly, not at all, or by being brusque or even brutal. Wives and husbands often refine this game of mutual rejection into a technique that destroys intimacy.

There are turndowns that avoid pointblank refusal (the "no thanks" or even "you must be kidding" variety) but are almost as hurtful. There's also the familiar, "Do you really want to?"—clearly inferring that while he may want to, you couldn't care less. Or, "I was sort of looking forward to watching that new show on television tonight," which relegates him and his desires to a lower scale than a situation comedy—a situation he won't find comical. Or, "Maybe later, hon, as soon as I finish doing the laundry," which puts his amorous suggestion on the level of your other domestic chores, and not even with top priority.

Avoid such turndowns. There is no place for them in any marriage that isn't practically in terminal condition. Sex is an area where the utmost in tact and diplomacy is called for, and these rebuffs are neither tactful nor diplomatic.

Does this mean you have no right to say "no" when you don't feel in the mood? Of course not. To make love when you don't feel like it leads to an unresponsiveness that can be an even worse form of rejection. Either partner in a marriage has to be free to say "no" as readily as "yes."

But usually it's more awkward for a woman to say "no." A woman may fear that if she says "no" now, her husband will say "no" later on or, even worse, say "yes" to someone else. A man identifies his sexual functioning with his power as a man, which means his ego is at stake.

What to do? First, make clear that you are rejecting this one invitation only. A good way is immediately to set up another date: "How about tomorrow when the children are at school?" or "Why don't we sneak away to a motel this weekend?" If your husband knows that you love him, admire him, and desire him, his ego isn't going to be impaired by an occasional refusal. What's important is to maintain sensual communication.

If you say "no" properly, it can be almost equivalent to saying "yes."

Body Language

One of the most frequent sources of friction between married couples is "temporary sexual incompatibility." There are certain times when one partner or the other is not in the mood, and these times have to be respected. You have to know when the auspices are right—or wrong.

How? One way is to learn to read body language. If one partner tries to cuddle up and the other moves away, or if one tries to embrace and the other stands as stiff as a board, or if one retreats behind a newspaper or magazine or book when the other approaches, you don't need a course in Berlitz to interpret what's being said.

At other times, vague messages are transmitted in body attitudes. You should try to become adept in reading these. Everyone has special idiosyncratic ways of conveying meaning via body movement. You should keep a special eye and ear alert for your partner's. A husband who sits in a hunched position with a frown may be saying, "Why don't you go away and leave me alone?" A husband who is fussing with the paper or some mechanical chore, making too many unnecessary motions, may be saying, "Don't bother me now. I'm *busy!*" And if he is standing or sitting rigidly, with arms folded, he is not a likely candidate for amorous play.

Psychologists researching this fascinating subject have learned that they can tell which are happy, *communicating* couples, and which are not, simply by observing videotapes of their behavior. The tapes carry no sound at all, so the researchers do not know what is being said. But happy couples tend to sit closer together, touch each other more, even seem to reach out to each other with gestures when speaking. They maintain eye contact for longer periods, and in general are more relaxed. Unhappy, noncommunicating couples usually sit near the edges of their chair—as if ready to get up and leave at short notice. They look at each other infrequently, hardly ever touch, speak from within themselves without reaching-out gestures, and often sit with their arms or legs defensively crossed.

Body language is such a good indicator of meaning that in many instances it can be relied on more than language itself. If you ask your husband to do something, and he replies with an automatic, "Yes, dear," while his body posture tightens or he looks up out of the corners of his eyes without turning to look at you directly, forget the actual words he is saying, and take my word for it: he means no.

At first, you may have difficulty in picking up nonverbal clues. But if you practice consciously, as often as you think to do it, you're certain to refine your skills. You will develop the kind of sensitive intimacy that sociologists call "interpersonal competence." You're also likely to prevent any number of unnecessary minor confrontations, covering the spectrum from the mildly unpleasant to the truly wounding.

Most important, you will be closing the emotional gap between you and your husband—and that is a long step forward on the road to true intimacy in marriage.

90° On Cuddling

How about those differences between your mood and your husband's on the important question of who wants to do what, and when? Neither of you is willing to be dominated by the other's desires, or to have your wants swallowed up by the other's demands. You'd like a way in which to assert a claim to your own emotional territory without shutting out your partner.

A method I call the Centigrade Test works for Bill and me.

As you know, centigrade is a method of measuring temperature that runs from 0 degrees, the extreme at which water freezes, to 100 degrees, the extreme at which water boils.

For example, the other evening Bill suggested enthusiastically that we have a nice brisk game of ping pong. I knew what he meant. Not long before, we had enjoyed playing ping pong in the nude. (Neither of us stayed to play out the full 21 points.)

However, on this particular evening, I had spent a long day in the library doing research, had done a large marketing, had cooked dinner, and was enjoying a glass of wine and lazily looking forward to a quiet, unathletic evening just sitting around listening to music.

So, without having to weigh Bill's offer too much, I said, "I'd put that around 20 degrees. How about Scrabble?"

"No better than 30 degrees."

"I'm 90 on cuddling, having more wine, and listening to that new Bach record I bought."

"I could get up to about 60 on that. How about Zinka Milanov instead?"

We compromised, since I was 70 on Zinka, and the evening ended up as satisfactorily as if we'd both been up for a go at ping pong. The advantage of the Centigrade Test is that you are able to express gradations of your real feeling. With the Centigrade Test, you can avoid saying a flat "no" to the basic question and say "no" only to the particular approach or activity. And that will help you avoid a lot of senseless quarrels.

Exhausted Gladiators

How does one go about having a "constructive" argument? Are there any ground rules?

There are.

AVOID CRUDE SLUGGING

It was fun watching the film *Who's Afraid of Virginia Woolf?* because we could share vicariously in the blows being dealt without feeling the wounds. In real life, when you start cutting each other verbally, you leave emotional scars. The mark of crude slugging is the non sequitur.

An example:

HE: Why is dinner so late?

SHE: I had to go back to the supermarket. I forgot to buy some things I needed.

HE: Can't you remember to do anything right the first time?

SHE: It so happens one of the things I forgot is beer. If you wouldn't drink so much, maybe your belly wouldn't look like a basketball.

HE: Look who's talking. If you put on any more weight, you'll have to get license plates.

SHE: You take after your father. He's as big a slob as you are.

HE: My father worked hard all his life. He didn't sit on his rump like your Dad. And he never ran around with women either.

SHE: Who the hell would run around with *you*?

HE: Maybe you'd like to know. Well, maybe I'll tell you. . . .

And so on until, like two exhausted gladiators, they can strike no more blows but simply glare at each other. Nothing has been accomplished except the laying on of wounds.

NEVER FIGHT TO A FINISH

Every argument is about something—even when, as in the example above, it has little to do with what is being said. The husband in that foolish slugfest might have complained about dinner being late because he was hungry or tired, had a bad day at work, or because he suspected his wife of simply not caring enough about him. She, in turn, might have been feeling tired because this was her cleaning day, the children had been impossible, or she resented the fact that her husband wasn't helping enough in the kitchen. These feelings would be the actual content of the argument.

In constructive arguing, the debate is limited to the genuine immediate problem and is not allowed to escalate into tribal warfare. A skirmish should not be extended to a battle, nor a battle to a war. Once that kind of progression is permitted, the result, in human as in national affairs, is to employ nuclear weapons. At Armageddon there are no victors. There *is* a loser, though. Your marriage. So define what it is you are arguing about, and stick to that.

DON'T BEAT AROUND THE BUSH

Come to the point quickly. Don't travel by way of the South Pole.

"I had a nice long talk with Freddie today. You know, that nice young man at the gas station I always thought was so shy. At least, everyone says so. I couldn't stop him from talking. It was almost embarrassing, the other cars lining up to get gasoline and him hanging in the window of my car and talking."

She knows perfectly well that her husband doesn't care to hear about young Freddie at the gas station. But she is 38 years old and he forgot to give her a birthday present last week. She'd like him to know she's still attractive to young men and he'd better not take her for granted.

AVOID SARCASM

A sharp-tongued woman of my acquaintance was hostessing a dinner party for another couple and Bill and myself. She brought the conversation around to her favorite subject—sex.

"Did you ever hear of a woman being convicted of rape? That isn't possible, is it, I mean with a man? Don't men have to be self-starters? Or so I've heard."

Obviously, the remark was aimed at her husband. Putting it in the form of sarcasm gave him a chance to reply in kind, and he did. "My wife thinks I should chase her around the bedroom like Harpo Marx."

Later that night, I've no doubt, both went to bed mad—and unsatisfied. Nothing was accomplished except to persuade at least two guests to avoid future dinners at their home.

The tendency to employ sarcasm as a method of discussion extends into many areas of life. Not long ago, I heard a woman tell her husband, "It's going to be cold this weekend. Do you think you could wrench yourself out of your easy chair and put up the storm windows? We don't need the screens any more. All the mosquitoes have frozen to death in their little igloos."

As an occasional verbal tool, sarcasm has its place. As a basic way of communication, it's destructive.

FIND THE RIGHT LEVEL OF COMMUNICATION

Oddly enough, sarcasm is sometimes used because a person is afraid of having an open argument, but in that event the fear of arguing is worse than arguing. You have to find the right level of argument. It's much better to say directly what's on your mind. "Look, I've been meaning to talk to you about. . . ." Or, "You know, I think we have a problem. I'd like to discuss it, and this seems as good a chance as any." Set a tone of rational discussion, and you may avoid the argument altogether. Your husband may try to prove he's as reasonable and as willing to discuss things as you are.

However, if argument does begin, there are a couple of guidelines that will help you to recognize when you're straying off the point, or shedding more heat than light, or drifting into personalities and away from the immediate subject.

When either starts saying, "I don't understand what *you've* got to complain about . . ." that's a warning signal. It's also a warning when either starts ridiculing: Ridicule is a signal that you've switched from constructive argument to destructive personal attack.

If you suddenly realize that the conversation is going around and around the same circle like a carousel, that you're saying the same things for the second and third time, it's time to cut the argument off at the impasse. You're not accomplishing anything. A possible cure: get away from generalities and back to specifics. Don't tell him how he's neglecting you and the children. Tell him that when he comes home from work you wish he wouldn't go right in and turn on the TV without saying hello, kissing you, and spending a little time with the children.

PUT IN A GRACIOUS WORD

The late Adlai Stevenson said it is better to light a candle than to curse the darkness. When you're both cursing the darkness, try to light a candle by saying something positive. Not every argument will present such an opportunity, but actively seek out the possibility. In the middle of a quarrel, you may not be in a frame of mind to hand out compliments, but you can make an effort to say something gracious that will deescalate the argument. The other evening, Bill and I were at a dinner party. He interrupted me in the middle of telling a story, and then ignored my (admittedly) sharp rebuke and went on with his topic. Driving home in the car, I told him how much I resented his behavior. Our quarrel escalated, until it seemed we were on the brink of a really serious conflict.

Suddenly I asked myself, why am I doing this? I was upset with Bill, yes, even more upset by his obstinacy in not conceding he had been wrong. But this was only one incident in a marriage that consisted of many, many pleasant occasions. So I told Bill, "Well, this was one time I just didn't like you very much, but basically I love you—and nothing can change that!"

Instantly, the dispute ended. "I love you too," Bill said quietly. He then apologized for interrupting me at the dinner table, explaining he hadn't really been listening when I began telling my story so he didn't realize he was interrupting. What had really angered him was my sharp response in front of other guests at the table. I was willing to admit I'd been wrong about that. A potentially serious marital conflict was avoided—because I found a way to put in a gracious word at the right time.

RING THE BELL

As I said before, an argument should never develop into a fight to the finish. A knockout is not your goal. When the round is over, stop fighting. You may be surprised to discover how much has already been accomplished by airing your differences.

YOU WIN—IF YOU KNOW HOW TO LOSE

During many interviews with happily married people, I discovered that a substantial number trace their present happiness to having thrashed out some problem in an emotional confrontation. A problem can exist for years while it is being denied, ignored, or simply misunderstood.

A self-centered lover thinks of marriage as some sort of competitive game—a kind of eenie, meenie, mynie, *me*—in which the right tactics and strategies will produce victory. But cooperation is the name of the marital game, and that is true even in argument.

One couple devised a strategy that is extremely simple, yet manages to bring most of their disputes to a quick and more satisfactory ending. When one thinks the other has made a convincing point, she or he says "Bingo!"

The simple tactic has profound results. No argument ever gets too heated, because the "Bingos" ensure that someone is having his or her reasoning carefully evaluated. The argument becomes a kind of game in which each tries to score as many "Bingos" as possible. This demands concentration on the concrete issue. It also has the effect of making each listen more carefully, instead of merely thinking about his or her debating points. Hearing the other person out with genuine attention goes a long way toward cooling off tempers.

There can be delight in actually losing an argument. Only inflexible or insensitive persons are unable to admit when they are on the wrong side of a debate. My friend Kate believes that strongly. She cut a small square from a white handkerchief and put it into a stand. That's her Truce Flag, which she keeps in a drawer of the night table. When either she or her husband Alan realizes that one has been mistaken in an argument, they get out the Truce Flag and display it where the other will be sure to see it. On the flag, Kate has lettered in red ink the oft-quoted *Love Means Never Having To Say You're Sorry*. "So far, it's worked 100 percent of the time. I guess it shows that in an argument between two people who love each other, a little humor can go a long way!"

The true purpose of argument is not to win, but to reconcile. There is always some right and wrong on both sides. When you concede the amount of truth that is on the other side, you are likely to gain a concession as to the amount of truth that is on your side.

NEVER LET THE SUN SET ON AN ARGUMENT

That may sound familiar. But cliches often get to be cliches because they contain a truth worth repeating. The wisdom that has made this piece of homely advice survive is still present. Don't let an argument go on and on, with no real ending. Don't go off on a new tangent and prolong the conflict unnecessarily.

Renewing an argument is fruitless. Yet I know couples who have managed to sustain the same argument for months, even years. They work up so many lines of controversy, points of altercation, areas of dispute, so expand the initial boundaries of contention, that there is no way the argument can ever end. Even if they wanted to, they could not simply call it off. They would have to sign a treaty.

No argument should persist for 24 hours. If it does, time will be working against a resolution. Does that mean all your arguing has solved nothing? Not necessarily. At least you've learned each other's point of view. No one who listens is immune to what is heard. In that fact lies your best hope for an eventual compromise.

Finally, here are four useful tips on how to use anger constructively.

First: Analyze what the real argument is about. Are you really mad because your husband had a bit too much to drink at that cocktail party, or because he was paying too much attention to that attractive young blonde and too little to you?

Second: Don't throw an old shoe into the boiling pot. If you are hotly debating whether to visit your mother at Thanksgiving or to spend the day at his brother's house with their family, you only cause the boiling pot to spill over by tossing in: "And, besides, you're not going to get me on a long car trip until you get snow tires. You promised you would two weeks ago. And I nearly got stuck on my way to the supermarket. . . ."

Third: Bear in mind that any argument has to have two sides, even as it has to have two people. Listen carefully to what he has to say, and let him speak until he's finished. Don't interrupt to correct or lecture or scold. Don't seize on some minor point as a desperate criminal might seize on a weapon. He has a right to get rid of his anger too, and interrupting will only make him angrier.

Fourth: Make up. Don't wait for him to apologize. That doesn't mean you have to say you were wrong. It's possible to agree to disagree. What you're likely to get back is gratitude—and love. If making up is hard to do while you're in a rage, wait until your anger cools. But don't wait too long. Sensuality can cool too.

PART
III

HONEYMOONING
FOR
LIFE

Starting Over

During lunch one day at the Metropolitan Museum of Art, in that lovely cafeteria by the pool, my friend Janice suddenly began telling me about her marriage. She and Ben had been married 14 years. And Ben had just told her he thought it was time for their marriage "to take a new direction." Ben, who was then 38, said he wanted to be free to date other women. He said the plain truth was that Janice did not excite him anymore, although he was fond of her and did not necessarily want a divorce. "Unless either of us finds someone else."

"I can't understand what brought it on," Janice told me. "Ben and I have always had a wonderful sex relationship. I was one of that vanishing breed of women who saved myself for the Big Night, when there would be no fear of interruption, no guilt, and we'd have the full blessing of the Establishment. It all couldn't have been better. That first night I reached orgasm and nine times out of ten since. I enjoy having sex with him, and I thought he enjoyed it with me. Is this what happens to all men after they've been married awhile?"

"I Don't Have A Lot To Lose"

Janice was not impressed when I told her about what I call the Sensuality Approach, and what it had done for me and for other women. But she heard me out, and finally agreed to try it. "I don't have a lot to lose. If Ben starts seeing other women—and I start dating other men—our marriage is as good as over anyway."

One morning a few weeks later, Janice telephoned to tell me that she and Ben were going to St. Thomas in the Virgin Islands for the winter. She sounded positively bubbly.

"What about Ben's business?" I asked, being as discreetly indirect as I could be. "Can he afford to be away that long?"

"He says it's time to find out if these people he's hired are any good. After all, they can't wreck the business, and he says he wants to get alone with me on some tropical island so he can get better acquainted with this fantastic woman he's married!"

"It sounds as if you don't have much of a problem with Ben anymore."

"I owe you a lot. You not only helped me to see my situation in a new light—but you gave Ben and me a way to reach out to each other."

Something A Little Vulgar

By now, I'm convinced that most marriages seldom come to an end because there is no life left in them. Marriages wilt and wither because the partners don't understand how much loving attention and effort must go into keeping a sensual relationship flourishing. As with friendships—so with love—there must be nurturing to sustain life. A marriage is not a piece of paper. It is a living thing that must receive the same careful and continual care that a gardener would give to a prize orchid. As a plant needs water, a marriage needs sensuality.

Let me tell you two true stories about people I know. When I advocated sensuality as a cure for what ailed her 22-year-old marriage, my friend Amanda was a little shocked. Somehow that idea didn't go with being married. "Marriage isn't *like* that," were her exact words.

Her marital complaint was familiar: another woman. Amanda didn't know who the woman was, and in her secret heart she didn't want to know. But she was certain there was someone, or why was Ralph having a suspicious number of late evening business dinners and conferences in town?

It took a while to persuade Amanda to try sensuality. The mere thought embarrassed her. Besides, Ralph would think her "peculiar," to say the least. After 22 years of marriage, a man doesn't expect his wife to come up with surprises. She knew what kind of man Ralph was, and I didn't. And so forth.

Taking the 5:10 Home

I suggested that perhaps Ralph might be a little surprised at first, but in the long run would be pleased. What won the day was the question I asked her about how "sensual" she rated Ralph on their honeymoon. I knew the answer from the look in her eyes before she said, "Very." Then the sensuality is still there, I told her, buried under years of perfunctory behavior. You've got to find it and regenerate it.

She carried the message home with her. Within a few months, Ralph was catching the 5:10 train home at night instead of the 7:40. And he never had to "stay in town to have dinner with some of the boys at the office." Amanda agreed that he was a very sensual man who had simply been repressed by her own lack of interest in him.

As for the other woman, if there was one, nothing was ever heard of her.

Moral: When you weigh your man in the balance, be sure your own thumb isn't on the scale.

Amanda, at the beginning of her program to restore sensuality to her marriage, wrote a list of marital maxims for herself to follow. Taken as a whole, they are a pretty good description of a truly sensual woman. With her permission, I offer her list here.

I Am Going To Try My Very Best To:

1. Be as alluring as I was on our honeymoon.
2. Be as understanding as I was when Ralph was having serious business problems.
3. Be as open and as accepting as I was when he told me about the love affairs he had before we were married.
4. Be as trusting as I was when he made that six-week business trip to Japan without me.
5. Be as honest about my feelings as I can—without making him feel under criticism.
6. Be respectful of his privacy.
7. Be ready to share, without demanding payment in kind.
8. Be willing to change and grow.
9. Be ready to live with him if he wants me, but without him if I have to.
10. Be ready to offer him the kind of love that gives him strength, but still allows him to be free.

I think that's a pretty good list, and I'm not surprised that the maxims worked. They worked because Amanda's change in attitude led to a corresponding change in Ralph. This point needs to be emphasized: You can't change anyone but yourself. If your marriage basically has enough going for it, the result of yur change in attitude will cause a growth in understanding on your husband's part also. Action and reaction is as inevitable in emotional relationships as in physics.

Not a Complete Woman

Eva had a very serious impediment to overcome in her marriage. She'd had a modified radical mastectomy, in which one breast and the lymph nodes under one arm were removed. Her physical recovery was complete, but emotionally she was still scarred. She didn't feel attractive to her husband Brad anymore. She told me he behaved differently to her. At night, he deliberately averted his eyes when she was undressing. Often he stayed out of the bedroom until she was in her night clothes and in bed. During the day, he avoided touching her or hugging her. They had used to enjoy kissing and holding each other close, but now his kisses were perfunctory and there was no other body contact.

"Brad can't bear to look at me," Eva said. "Obviously, I repel him. We have no sex life at all. He always huddles over on his side of the bed."

"What's your reaction to that?" I asked.

"I've got to face it. Our marriage isn't working. I don't know how to make him desire me any more, the way I am."

"The way you are?"

"Why should he, or any man for that matter, want someone who isn't a complete woman?"

"Do you blame yourself for what's happened? It isn't your fault. If Brad acts as though it is, you have every right to be angry with him."

"Angry?"

"If he avoids physical contact with you, he's responsible for making you feel less than a woman. He ought to be ashamed of himself. I have a friend who's getting married next week, and she had a double mastectomy."

"You mean, she's getting married after she had an operation like *that*?"

"Apparently you assume a man can't fall in love with a woman in that condition. There may be some men who are like that, but not many. What they'd be saying, in effect, is that they can fall in love with one part of a woman's body but not with her. If you'd lost a foot or a hand or had your appendix taken out, would you expect Brad to fall out of love with you?"

"That's different."

"I want you to try something. I want you to be the most loving, warm, *sensual* person you can be. Invite him to make love to you—if not in words, then by being as seductive as you've ever been toward him."

"That would be ridiculous—the way I am now. . . ."

"Try."

Eva did try. When I met her again two weeks later she was looking radiant.

"I've been several different kinds of a fool, and I admit it," she said. "Whatever gave me the idea that an operation could somehow ruin everything that was between us?"

Pent-up Emotions

The night Eva began to come out of her imposed shell, she had served a special candlelight dinner, with wine, and sat with Brad listening to "Brigadoon," their favorite musical. She cuddled up close, and when he started to draw back, said, "Oh, no, please, darling. Put your arm around me."

"But I'm afraid I might hurt you," he replied.

And then, as if on the same impulse, they began talking about the pent-up emotions that had been isolating them from each other. Brad was almost in tears. It turned out that he had been afraid to touch her since a day soon after the operation when he had tried to hug her and her wince of pain warned him to stop. He had not realized that the incision would be so tender. His forgetfulness made him feel like a brute. He had overreacted, deciding he would not touch or try to caress her again until she told him it was all right.

That was why he had not given her more than a perfunctory kiss and why at night he huddled over on his side of the bed. The reason he averted his eyes when she was undressing? He didn't want to embarrass her.

"I'd gotten everything completely backwards," Eva told me. "I wanted to believe he loved me, but it was too hard because I felt so maimed. I couldn't help being aware of that empty place where my breast had been. I really wanted to be close to him, and it hurt when he turned away. It just never occurred to me that *I* was the one turning away. Or that *I* might be the reason for his apparent lack of interest. My talk with you helped turn my attitude around. When I think of the torment I went through, I feel so sorry for all the couples who suffer separately and in silence. If they just had the courage to try, they might put an end to their pain. It's a terrible waste of feeling, a *starvation* of feeling."

Our opinion of love derives from our first experiences with it, and influences us throughout adult life. In Eva's case, she had discovered that the way to earn her parents' love and approval was to "look nice." For her, love became overly dependent on the external factor of physical appearance.

Much of the trouble we get into is because we continue, at least in some degree, to look at emotional relationships in an immature and childish way. Each of us uses past experience to interpret each new situation—which may be normal and healthy. But sometimes old concepts blind us to new possibilities, and lead us to repeat self-defeating behavior.

Keeping In Touch

Here's a practical way to check on the level of sensual communication in your marriage: Schedule a regular meeting with your husband to review the progress of your emotional relationship.

This method may not work for everyone, nor is it needed by every couple. But if it appeals to you—and if you have a cooperative husband—it's a good idea.

Choose a convenient time in which you can go over the events of the past week and discuss problems and questions that have come up. You might have informal notes that make a kind of agenda. A businesslike approach to emotional concerns has a cooling effect. It tends to keep the volatile content of the discussion at a stable level.

For example, your notes might begin with minor annoyances of the week: Why did you wait so long to mail off that wedding present? How come you forgot to make a dentist appointment for the children? Why did you promise to take Danny to the Little League game and then work too late at the office?

This can be balanced with minor successes: how you persuaded a neighbor to do something about that incessantly barking dog; how well the new recipe for ratatouille worked out; how pleased Danny was with his new baseball glove. You should include things that amused you also: an unintentionally funny newspaper ad *(Sale! TV Sets! Only Used in Hotel Rooms At Fantastic Prices!)*, or an intentionally funny cartoon (scientists looking through a microscope at the beginning of a human reproductive cell: "Look! She's giving him an apple!").

Your weekly review should then move on to more

serious problems and concerns. Anything that really bothers you can be on this agenda. The problems can range from why he brought home two people from the office unexpectedly for dinner, to why you were unresponsive when he was in an amorous mood Tuesday night.

Here, you are on more difficult emotional terrain, so proceed cautiously. A couple of hints may help: Try to be temperate, logical, and fair-minded; always be candid, and feel free to discuss any impression or grievance. Most important is not the exact messages you are giving, but the fact that you are holding a meeting in which you are at full liberty to discuss such matters. To paraphrase Marshall McLuhan, the meeting itself is the message.

The meeting should last about an hour. That's enough time to go over the week's events and to expand on subjects that most interest you. Less time is likely to result in a too shallow or hasty summary. More time is an invitation to prolong the discussion into a real debate.

These weekly meetings are likely to be most rewarding if the attitude of both partners is mutually helpful. And remember: You are not exchanging complaints, you're helping each other over difficulties, reaching a better understanding.

A meeting should never result in either partner accepting blame with a show of bravery—and inward resentment. And neither should ever consider criticism an attack on her or his self-esteem.

Try your best during these discussions to be cheerful and optimistic. You're solving problems, not rehearsing them. Never pursue a topic, but trust it to make its own impact. Stretch your mind and be creative in looking for solutions. This is an opportunity for both of you; you don't want it to pass without making an improvement in your relationship to each other, no matter how minor. Look at it not as a chore but as a challenge, a small constructive reevaluation. It should and will increase emotional rapport.

Those who adopt this weekly review report that it has not only helped them to discharge pet peeves and share pleasures, but to come to a richer participation in each other's lives. They also discover that it is possible to experience minor annoyance with a person without in any way endangering your love.

The technique is useful for couples who are just married and want to maintain their honeymoon glow—and for those married for years who want to make contact with each other again.

Eleanor Was the First

Eleanor is a career woman who has never been very attractive. In college—when all the girls were dating and she wasn't—she decided to concentrate on a career instead of marriage. By the time she was 34, she was vice president of a large department store. That was the only vice Eleanor ever got acquainted with. She wasn't a virgin; she'd had one brief affair in her senior year of college. That experience convinced her that giving up sex was not the hardest decision she would ever have to make. In fact, giving up sex was like giving up armadillo steak—she hadn't liked it much anyway.

Then she met Colin, a successful lawyer, very active in civil liberties. After a few dates, he told Eleanor he'd fallen in love with her, "because you're the smartest woman I know and never try to use the fact that you're a woman to gain advantage." They were married. Colin proved to be as aggressive beneath the sheets as in his law office. He was enchanted with Eleanor's responsiveness. For her, the relationship had a dreamlike quality—she was half expecting to wake up one morning and find that Colin had never existed except in her dreams.

Today, they have a child and are the happiest couple you'd ever hope to meet. Eleanor does everything she can think of to please Colin, succeeds admirably, and is fully rewarded by his love and devotion.

So what did I have to teach Eleanor? You guessed it. Nothing. She was one of the first—no, she *was* the first—person I talked to about the secrets of the sensually married. I've used some of her tips in this book. If they aren't new to you, they certainly are to me!

In the course of interviewing many "honeymooners" enjoying lifetime marriages, I have picked up random observations that illustrate the countless small ways in which happily married people say "I love you" without actually using the words. I'm putting them down, in no particular order, directly from my notes.

Hints From Honeymooners

"She washes my hair for me every week. She says she loves to do it. I not only get the best shampoo going—but I love the feeling of her hands stroking me."

"He never complains when I serve him leftovers. He always says everything I cook tastes better the second time around, and praises me for my 'creative cookery.'"

"Whenever I admire some other woman's looks or figure, he always tells me what's wrong with her and why he likes me better."

"Today I tried—seriously tried—to think of any faults my wife has. And the only thing I could come up with is that she's a stickler for good table manners. I couldn't find anything else—and that's why I told her, 'What a prize I've got!'"

"There isn't anything my husband doesn't do well. He cooks better than I can, fixes anything that's broken, and is a marvelous host and the funniest storyteller in the world. If I tell him how marvelous he is, he tells me how much he envies my willpower because I quit smoking after being on two packs a day for years and because I can go on a diet and stay on it. I never pay him a compliment without his somehow turning it into a compliment for *me!*"

"He takes our two children out for long hours fishing—to give me a much needed rest from my chores. They clean their catch and bring it back and make a cookout, so I don't have to do a thing. I'm Queen for a Day!"

"She knows how to keep a sense of humor even under the worst kind of pressure—and she's taught me to do the same. She's the most precious gift life has brought me!"

"I have to be careful about saying what things I like, because he'll usually buy them for me. And he makes me feel like a *femme fatale*, even on the days when I'm looking like something no self-respecting cat would even bother to drag in."

"He calls from the office, twice a day usually. I know how busy he is and how he must plan for those calls so he won't be interrupted. But he never sounds hurried, and he's never broken off our call because of 'another call coming in' or for any other reason. It's silly of me to be flattered by that, but I just can't help it!"

"He remembers my birthday, our anniversary, my favorite flowers."

"She's very supportive when anything goes wrong, and she's always patient, even-tempered, and interested in anything I do that interests me."

This is the very stuff of which successful marriages are made. Small attentions keep true affection alive, when the job threatens to take over, or housekeeping takes over, or routine takes over, or when you begin to wonder where the romance went. A marriage can settle down to a dreadful condition in which, like that of a dermatologist's patient, it never dies but never gets better. Try some of these hints from honeymooners when days seem to move in a procession of loveless drudgery and there's nothing to look forward to except more of the same.

Rewarding Relationships

If everyone with a fading, lack-lustre, fatigued, or indifferent marriage would give sensuality half a chance, the transformations would be wondrous to behold—and to feel.

Among friends I've persuaded to try sensuality, there are many whose marriages were on the shoals and sinking fast. Nearly all of them are "honeymooners" today. You can be one too. George Bernard Shaw said that marriage will always be popular because it combines the maximum of temptation with the maximum of opportunity—and certainly that's how most people regard it when on their honeymoon. But then they lose sensuality along the way and, with it, the power to revitalize and strengthen their marriage.

There are many different kinds of sensual relationships; they run the gamut from brief social contacts to profound and meaningful intertwinings in which each person yields up part of her or himself. There are relationships based on a love of fun, need for emotional support, intellectual compatibility—even a kinship in politics! There are sadistic and masochistic combinations of every variety. And there are the most rewarding relationships, to which the partners bring their differing views of self and the world, and reconcile them in love.

You can test your attitudes about keeping sensuality alive in your marriage by indicating with a "yes" or "no" whether you agree or disagree with the following.

1. There is no happiness in marriage without self-respect and mutual trust.
2. If you expect displays of love when you're displaying selfishness, jealousy, irrational anger, and general sourness of disposition, you are going to be disappointed.
3. No marriage is perfect, and dissatisfactions need airing. You must be willing to risk openness.
4. Pure "giving" is not the soul of a real marriage. Each takes, each gives, at different times, and in material and emotional ways.
5. Much as you might think you want to, you and your mate will never merge into a single person. Wives and husbands will remain two people, not a single entity.
6. Be free to levy demands on your partner, but realize that she or he won't always be ready to yield.
7. A marriage that is based on sex is not a true union,

nor likely to endure. Real closeness demands more.

8. Much of the fault we find in others is a projection of what we feel about ourselves. When you ridicule your partner, you reveal dislike of yourself.

9. Boredom is a major cause of marital discontent and a more general cause of divorce than infidelity. To be happily married, you and your mate must keep finding new ways of expression and development.

10. Make your worst mistakes on your own, not in your marriage.

As you doubtless guessed, the "answer" to each of the foregoing statements is "yes." These are attitudes that keep sensuality intact and promote the chances for a long-term happy marriage.

The Best Is Yet To Be

All of us belong to the Now generation. All of us, of whatever age, are sharing the very same minute of time.

Queen Elizabeth I, on her deathbed, allegedly cried out, "Everything I possess for one more moment of life!" Yet here you are with numberless moments lying ahead of you, worried not about exchanging all you possess for a single moment more, but about how to cope with the numberless moments ahead.

"I can't believe I'm this old," a friend said to me the other day. "It must have happened very suddenly!"

For most of us, age arrives as a completely unexpected event. You've seen it coming but have put that particular reality away into the closet where you keep things you don't ever intend to look at again. One day, almost by accident, you open the closet and all your fears come tumbling out.

The Sea of Uncertainty

Lenore and Bernie, everyone agreed, were a happily married couple. Married 35 years, they were still affectionate and companionable, wonderfully adjusted to each other—real Honeymooners For Life.

Suddenly Lenore and Bernie were divorced.

No one could believe it, including me. Not long afterward, I sat and had coffee with Lenore in her kitchen, listening to her tell me that Bernie had gotten "involved in a love affair."

"Men prefer younger women, that's a fact," she said. "There's no way to compete when you get older."

If Lenore had bothered to look around her, she would have seen many wives coping with that "insoluble" problem. An older wife has many things going for her that no younger rival can possibly match. She has poise and experience, empathy and wisdom. She has a background of shared companionship and memories. These are advantages that can more than offset the sleek body of a younger woman.

Older men like to look at younger women, but I'm not sure they would know what to do with one. They have nothing in common. Even their sexual capacities are unequal, and will get more so. Men recognize this challenge, and fear the threat of increasing competition from younger men who have more physical appeal and more sexual energy and drive. What older man wants to cast himself adrift on such a sea of uncertainty?

Many older men do, not because their wives are no longer young, but because they have failed to maintain their sensual image. The process is as insidious as a slow-burning fire in the basement of a home. Suddenly the fire leaps up, and then it's too late to save anything. This is a parallel to what happens when a woman stops making an effort because she's "too old for that kind of nonsense."

"Nothing can wreck a good marriage," runs an old saying. But what *is* a good marriage? Try a sharper definition. "Nothing can wreck a marriage in which the partners fulfill each other's needs."

That is what a "good marriage" is all about. On the laundry list of needs for fulfilling, put sensuality at the top. When sensuality goes out of marriage, all that's left is the hulk—a working or living arrangement that habit has hardened into routine. This is what John Ciardi calls "the habituation of middle age." Nothing ever changes, all effort to improve is abandoned, and there is really nothing to look forward to. In such a marriage, the wife and husband hardly remember what needs they had.

Let's talk about what you can do to get the most out of what should be the golden honeymoon years of marriage—the years in which the two of you might feel as did the poet Robert Browning: "Grow old along with me, the best is yet to be."

Shape Up

When you look into a mirror, can you just barely make out the dim silhouette of the young person you once were? Start bringing that person back to life. There are all sorts of ways to do it, some of which I've previously mentioned. You can shape a new figure. Hair can be any shade you want it. Magic comes in bottles and jars, in wigs and at dress shops. "As age takes from you, I engraft you new," Shakespeare said. But today you don't have to rely on an indulgent lover's eyes to repair your failings. Betty Ford didn't.

The most stunning-looking older woman I know is now 70 years old. I've never heard any man describe Norma as anything but beautiful. Her Dresden-doll skin glows, and her green eyes shine with interest and excitement. Bill says her face seems to open like a flower when she looks up at him. She is remarkable, but she is also wise enough to use whatever help she can to enhance her beauty. Her spun-gold hair is perfectly done, her makeup skillfully applied, her best features (she has *gorgeous* eyes) artfully played up, her clothes expensive and perfectly suited to her figure, and she wears the most delicious perfumes. "Norma is an absolute marvel," said a friend of ours recently after attending a fabulous party at her home which, as usual, was perfectly prepared, hostessed and guested. "How does she do it?"

I asked her. She said, "I suppose I take a little extra

care. A little extra care can turn a pudding into zabaglione and pancakes into crepes suzettes—and a woman my age into someone considered attractive. Above all, I don't try to compete with younger women. I'd rather have someone think I'm beautiful for my age than pretend I'm 50 and have everyone think I'm certainly looking the worse for wear!"

Many men look attractive as they get older. Look at Gregory Peck. The craggier and shaggier he gets, the more interesting he is. An older man with a haggard, lined face can be fascinating because he looks as if he's *lived*. He obviously knows more about women and the world than a callow, unformed, young rival.

Older women can look fascinating too. Ingrid Bergman, Dinah Shore, Lauren Bacall, Sophia Loren, Gina Lollobrigida, Zsa Zsa Gabor, Anne Bancroft, and Ava Gardner are all between 45 and 60. But you still see men's heads turning to watch them admiringly. I was in a theater not long ago when Audrey Hepburn came in, and not a single male in the audience was looking at anyone else. Bill told me, "That's *real* glamor." Audrey hasn't lost any of her "star quality." Nor have Irene Dunne, Claudette Colbert, and Barbara Stanwyck—to name just three who are in their 70s and still going strong!

Be Interested

Elizabeth Taylor doesn't bother about dieting (and it shows) but neither does she worry about growing old and losing her looks. "Being middle-aged doesn't frighten me at all," she says. "I see wrinkles and double chins in the mirror, but what difference does it make? I earned them. I'll be a nice, cuddly, gray-haired old thing one day, but one thing I guarantee you: I won't act or feel that way. The way to stay young is to enjoy life!"

Even though we're not movie stars, there's no reason we can't carry our own "star quality" into our later years. My friend Dee is 42, has been married for 21 years, and her husband Tim swears that she looks better now than when he first met her. He brought out her early photographs to prove his point. At her high school graduation, Dee was a plump-faced, pretty girl, but not remarkably different from the other graduates. She hadn't yet found the sense of her own personal style. A quarter of a century later, Dee is an indisputably lovely woman.

Tim is enormously proud of her. "Some women in their 40s turn into Ma Kettle. They do the cooking, the cleaning, the shopping, and maybe look after kids. Important? Sure. But Dee was never willing to settle for that. She stayed an interesting person. She keeps up with everything that's going on. She's interested in politics, sports, books, music. She's always dragging me around to things. I grumble sometimes, but basically I love it."

Recently, Adeline and her husband Eric, a retired ad agency vice-president, booked passage on a trip to the Orient. That in itself would be an exciting enough adventure for almost anyone, but not for Adeline.

She's taking a course in Chinese so that they'll get more out of their brief stay in mainland China. When I pointed out that she'll be studying for months just to "get the most out of" five days, she answered with a smile, "But the studying won't be wasted. I'll be able to speak Chinese!"

A woman like that never has to worry about growing old.

Martha is 61, married for almost 40 years. For her wedding anniversary, she asked her husband Dan to get her a telescope to study the stars. She's reading books on astronomy, and has decided to go back to school in the fall and take up the study seriously.

Bill and I visited Martha and Dan just the other evening. The new telescope had just arrived. We spent a marvelous evening star-gazing, drinking wine, talking about some of the unsolved riddles of astronomy. Martha is another woman who will never be trapped in a cycle of deadening routine.

Be An Individual

Helen Gurley Brown, editor of *Cosmopolitan* magazine and a well-known author, married for the first time when she was 37 years old. What's more, she married one of the most eligible, attractive men in the country. David Brown was 44 years old, a top motion picture producer, literate, witty, extremely wealthy, and extremely bright. He was pursued by every bosomy young starlet in Hollywood and some bosomy leading ladies too. Yet Helen, who by her own admission is "not bosomy or beautiful or even pretty," was the one David chose. They have been honeymooning for more than 20 years.

How did she enchant a man whom so many younger, prettier women were after, and how has she managed to keep him happy all these years? "It wasn't a miracle," she says. "I *earned* him." He found her irresistible partly because she had sharpened her wits and learned to survive in the highly competitive world of magazine publishing. Also she had a glittering, glamorous image and was an independent person, neither an emotional sponger nor a financial one. She understood men. She didn't worry about losing him, because "while you do need a man every step of the way, they are often cheaper emotionally and a lot more fun by the dozen." A woman like Helen Gurley Brown is far more capable of completing a man's life than a younger, better-looking, but less colorful—and, fundamentally, less attractive—woman.

Lloyd is the husband of dynamic, 48-year-old Hilary, who runs a charity benefit business from her home. Lloyd told me that when he returns from work in the evening, Hilary is always at the door to greet him, "dressed to the nines and with an ice-cold martini in her hand. She has all kinds of news and gossip to share with me. I look forward to coming home. And she *looks* so great! I can't believe she's a mother and a grandmother. Incidentally, neither can her daughter!"

An older married woman has many advantages. The problems of home and family no longer occupy all her waking moments. She has time to read, to exercise, to go to the hairdresser, to shop, to whip up a perfectly delicious Beef Wellington for dinner. She can lunch with friends, go antiquing in the country, take a course, join the museum, attend a concert or a lecture, see a play. She can meet her husband for cocktails, keep up with *Time, Newsweek,* AND *U.S. News and World Report.* She can bone up on the stock market, or on the business her husband is in so that she can talk and listen intelligently about it or possibly be helpful. She can work part time for her husband if he owns the business, or she can take a job. She can sign up for dancing lessons or join a bowling league—with or without her husband. There is an infinite variety of activities she can pursue that will occupy the time she once had to devote to raising children, cooking three meals a day for who-knows-how-many, ironing and cleaning and picking up after everyone.

If, when she no longer has to, she holds to the same inflexible routine that she established during the early years of her marriage; if, like the Bourbons of France, she can learn nothing and forget nothing; and if, as a result, her husband ups and leaves her, she has no one to blame but herself.

More and more women have decided that the middle and late years of marriage are the sweetest. As a result, the older married woman is emerging as the newest of our glamor girls. But there are still far too many women "of a certain age" who have, in effect, written themselves off. They are brainwashed into the belief that there is nothing left for them but a humdrum existence in which they should count themselves lucky simply to be married, without worrying their heads about what quotient of happiness they may be deriving from their marriage.

Be Optimistic

Women who stay in a rut seem to think that no matter how fast the years are flying, their life is never going to change. So, they reason, they have plenty of time to stir themselves and climb out of their rut. Well, sooner or later, their life *will* change, if only because neither they nor their husbands are immortal. Suppose a husband dies. What then? An even drearier emptiness stretching ahead to the final horizon? A woman had better be prepared with some other alternatives for living.

Before a sudden crisis forces you to decide, try to think of what you would do if your husband had less than a year to live. I asked this question of women I interviewed, and a curious pattern developed. All the true honeymooners gave me upbeat answers.

Here are just a few:

"I'd ask for the name of another doctor."

"I would probably write a book about how we can all be happy in marriage, like you're doing. And let my husband read it."

"I'd take every last cent we had in the world and go off on one long glorious round-the-world binge."

"I don't think I'd tell anyone. And I'd try to make every single minute of his life more meaningful."

"I'd read all the books on life after death until I found one that would convince me."

"I'd ask him to start giving away possessions to people who would love them as much as he did. There's no satisfaction leaving things in a will. I'd like him to see people's pleasure while he's still around, and have the satisfaction of knowing that the things he loved would survive him."

"I'd make love a lot. If death is going to get him, I'd rather have it happen while he's making love to me in the back seat of a car."

Among women whose marriages were not so happy—even though, in many cases, they were more dependent on their husbands—these are typical answers:

"I'd probably kill myself."

"I'd get as many men as I could into my bed. I'd have to be *sure* he was going to die, though, or I wouldn't have the courage to do it."

"I'd stop worrying about how to keep him happy. By the time I found out the answer, it would be too late."

"I'd fall apart."

"I'd have a ball—and charge everything to my husband. Let them try to collect after he's gone!"

"I'd go on, just about the way I am now."

It isn't hard to see which group has the most constructive attitude, even when confronting the idea of death. If you were a man, from which group of women would you pick the likeliest prospects for a happy marriage?

Right.

That's how men feel about it too.

"I Can't Forgive Myself"

As women get older, they are often haunted by the ghost of failures past. If they mean to enjoy their golden honeymoon years, they have to banish these ghosts forever. They must free their energies and attention from the shackles of a past that is beyond changing. You want your entire being, your emotional and physical and spiritual selves to live and function now, in the present moment.

I'm sure you know older people who have allowed themselves to sink into a bottomless pit of remembered events, people, and places. At best, these kind of memories lead to nostalgic daydreaming; at worst, they can cripple you with remorse for opportunities missed, failures that might have been avoided if only. . . .

Let me tell you about Karen. Karen is a very attractive woman who had a troubled love affair with a married man. This man, the love of her life, whom she was unable to marry, had finally moved to another town. For three years Karen mourned him, meanwhile turning down dates with other eligible men. It was only her ex-lover she wanted when her fancy took flight from her real-life situation.

The Best Is Yet To Be

One day, Karen was at a party where the most attractive man present began paying marked attention to her. She couldn't understand why this good looking, charming, sophisticated man would bother with an insipid person like herself. *Why* was she insipid? Because she obviously had not been good enough to hold her married lover.

She finally began to date her new suitor. She saw him almost daily, but found it hard to believe that he was really interested in her. She was not his type—she was sensible, hard-working, practical, anything but glamorous. One day, when he was out of town, he sent a telegram: "I just can't stop thinking about you. Won't you take me out of my misery—and marry me?"

She did marry him and, as she puts it, "I became the most cherished woman in the world." But she wasn't happy. The memory of her former lover still haunted her. When she turned 30 she thought of him at 46, and when she was 35 she wondered how he looked now that he was past 50. Did he think about her? She had been a brief passing interlude in his life, but she would never forget him.

Then her former lover telephoned out of the blue. He was going to be in town for a few days and wondered if they could meet. She was so excited that she could hardly wait. On the appointed day, they met for lunch at his hotel. She saw this balding man with a decided paunch. He was not half as good looking as her husband, and he turned out to be not half as interesting nor nearly as much fun to be with.

He, however, told Karen that he still cared for her.

"You've always been my girl, you know." He said that his wife meant nothing to him, that he was planning to ask her for a divorce. Karen was relieved to be able to tell him that she no longer had any interest in marrying him because she was very happily married to a man she adored. He lowered his head as if she had struck him, and muttered something about how he had always known she was too good for him.

"I can't forgive myself for all those wasted years," Karen told me. "I let an old memory cast an evil spell over my life. And so I never realized how happy I was."

We all live in houses of memory inhabited by ghosts, and like frightened children we still react. They can paralyze us, make us unable to enjoy ourselves as we would like to in the present—the only time we ever have.

The Scrooge Solution

Some older women are inhibited from leading full, free, sensual lives by the fear of age alone. Even if they are in good health, they count the few years that may remain to them. This kind of anxiety accelerates the aging process. Women of 50 can enjoy their sensual power fully as much as they did when they were younger, but we all know women of 50 who seem to have been overtaken prematurely by age.

For such people, there is a cure. I call it the Scrooge

Solution. You remember in Charles Dickens's *A Christmas Carol*, the miserly rapscallion Scrooge is given a glimpse of the future, with Scrooge himself dead. And that glimpse sets in motion his transformation to a man capable of enjoying life and bringing pleasure to others.

The Scrooge Solution is a marvelous fantasy game that can bring you to a renewed appreciation of life. Approach it in perfect seriousness, as you might a session with a psychoanalyst.

Turn off all the lights in a room, or leave them very low. Lie down on a sofa or on a bed, and close your eyes. Now, beginning with your lower extremities, command the life to go out of them. Picture the blood circulation as slowing down and stopping. Do the same farther up your body. Imagine as vividly as you possibly can the growing numbness that is creeping up. Do not move a muscle. Your body should be totally passive, unable to resist the relentless advance of lifelessness. Imagine that the coldness has reached your throat, that you cannot speak. Now it has reached your eyes. You cannot open them. You are out of your body.

In the darkness, imprint on your mind this scene. The door opens, and one by one the people enter who would be present at your funeral. Examine the faces of the mourners who gather around your body. What would you give just to be able to speak to them, to touch them? But you cannot. There were so many things left unsaid, weren't there? So many kindnesses you wished you had done. Wouldn't it be sweet if you could tell these people how important they were to you—as, by their tears, they are now showing how important you were to them?

Now fix upon one face—your husband's. This is a face you have known in many moods. You will never look at it again. Never. You will never feel his strong arms holding you or his kiss. Remember the times you have made love. Choose a single time when everything was particularly tender, when you were so closely wrapped in each other that you felt as if you had truly become one person.

How you planned for the years together! But you never learned to live for the minutes. You let yourself drag through minutes that became hours and hours that became days without realizing how precious the time was. Time is gone now, irrecoverable. If you could only tell him how much you loved him.

But you aren't dead! You're alive. Let life surge slowly back into your body. Let the warm rush of feeling return to your limbs, to your body, your chest, your throat. You can speak again! You can say all those things you always meant to say. You can still touch those you love. You can know again the joy of being loved.

Sit up and look at the darkness around you for one more second, remembering what it was like to be dead. Then turn on the light.

Isn't life *beautiful?*

Problems which seemed too much for you to cope with, angers which seemed to be slowly throttling you, decisions that seemed impossible to make—how much simpler everything now seems.

I recommend the Scrooge Solution whenever you are in doubt as to the value of your life. At any age, life is a blessing for which we must remind ourselves to be grateful. Refuse to accept anything that inhibits your pleasure in being alive—old memories, old age, or old rancors. These are what limit your potential for living—and loving.

An Unfinished Product

"The real tragedy," Sigmund Freud said, "is when a man outlives his body."

An equal tragedy for women too, as the great man would agree. But the tragedy of outliving love, outliving the ability to experience it to the fullest, is the greatest tragedy of all.

Don't pigeonhole yourself. In sensual terms, you are not a Finished Product in any sense. If you find yourself saying, "I can't help it, that's the way I am," stop at once. Don't accept yourself as someone too old to be capable of change. Remember that when change stops, for practical purposes the individual ceases to exist. Life *is* change.

I know a woman who gets upset at almost every little thing that happens. Not only is she continuously simmering with resentment over something her husband either has or hasn't done, but sooner or later she quarrels with every person she knows. She blames her "sensitive" nature. "I've always been like that," she says. "I'm sensitive, and there's nothing I can do about it."

In the first place, she is not "sensitive" at all. She's touchy. Truly sensitive people are aware of other people's feelings besides their own. In the second place, by pigeonholing herself, saying that she can't change, she becomes a Finished Product. There is no further place to go except to the grave.

Pigeonholing

Bill and I went to Europe with a couple we liked, although we knew them to be inflexible people. In Paris, George insisted on devoting part of every day to visiting a different wing of the Louvre. Bill and I, having been to the Louvre, wanted to see other sights. We wanted to walk the Paris streets, stop in sidewalk cafes and just watch people passing by. The other couple's rigid itinerary did not allow for unscheduled pleasures of any kind.

One day, we crossed a small bridge over the Seine and saw a knot of people looking down at the embankment below, where a group of young musicians were having the time of their lives. They were giving an impromptu concert, marching alone Indian file, up and down the stairs, playing wild, free improvisational jazz. Everyone in the steadily-growing crowd was delighted. Bill and I stopped to watch.

George said, "We really should be on our way."

"There's plenty of time," Bill said. "Joanna and I are going to watch awhile."

George shook his head reprovingly. "I don't think you ought to encourage them. They're not *serious* musicians."

Isn't it sad that there are people like George and Paulette who think that music should only be played by "serious" musicians? The kind of music that delights both the players and the audience, that transfigures a moment of living, has no place in their scheme of things. They actually shut themselves off from enjoying new sensations, and therefore from sensuality itself.

That is the danger of pigeonholing. Once you pigeonhole an experience you don't have to bother with it any more. You can mount a butterfly under glass, but you will never know the joy of watching that butterfly in flight.

When you say you're "too old for that sort of thing," whether "that sort of thing" means passion or public speaking, it's a way of removing yourself from a whole category of activities. The more categories you remove yourself from, the more limited your life becomes.

Start movement going the other way. Deliberately seek out new experiences, and make a definite effort to understand and appreciate them. That goes for anything from rock music to rollerskating, from birdwatching to belly dancing. These are all activities that "connect" you to the ongoing experience we call life.

The more connections you make between you and life, the younger you will act and feel.

"I've Got To Be Me!"

Many surveys show that older people are having sexual relations more frequently, and at a much more advanced age, than hitherto suspected. There is no set number of times a week for a married couple at any age. There is no standard, no average, no outside compulsion on them to perform or not to perform. There is only desire—and satisfaction.

Stella was 44 when she began having symptoms of menopause. At first she thought, Well, that settles it. I'm definitely getting old. To her surprise, however, she began to want sex more than before. Her husband Roger had a regular schedule—sex on Saturdays.

She tried to break the routine, making tentative approaches. He declined, gently but firmly. "You know, I'm not getting any younger," he said. "You can't expect me to perform like a young stud."

As Masters and Johnson have shown, the more a couple engages in sex the more their capacity to enjoy sex increases. Fortunately, Stella was able to convince Roger to try. They experimented with different techniques and positions, and broke out of their Saturday syndrome. They began to regulate their sex life not by the day of the week, but by their inclinations—by the pulse rather than the calendar.

The change was just what Roger needed. Later, he

admitted to Stella that he had really been afraid he would not be able to keep up with her. With a reinvigorated sex life, he felt like a new man, more optimistic about himself and his future.

Lately, Stella has added a new variation. She and Roger both write down on several slips of paper the different ways in which they would like to make love. These are put into a bowl, and one or the other gets first draw. This has introduced more variety and spontaneity into their sexual lives. Neither is allowed to fall into the rigid pattern of, "oh, no, I don't like to do that." As long as one partner wants it, the other must at least be willing to give it a try.

Of course it is possible for a married couple to have unequal sexual needs—particularly as they grow older. Markyta told me that her husband, who was 48, suddenly announced to her that he didn't want to have sex more than twice a month. "I'm two years older than he is," she said, "and I'm not ready to semi-retire. But what can I do? Start having affairs?"

Her case is fairly typical of many women whose husbands have entered their later years. Just as the woman is getting more interested in sex, their husbands start to lose interest. A 50-year-old woman is waxing when her husband is waning. However, most of the time the man's trouble is psychological rather than physical. In midlife, a man often suffers a kind of male menopause. He becomes aware of aging and is depressed at the way time is running out. He begins to worry about his sexual attractiveness and, inevitably, his potency. An episode of impotence will so alarm him that he will try to avoid further embarrassment by reducing the number of challenges he has to meet.

What can you do? Be sympathetic, understanding, don't make demands, and—above all—build up his confidence. Show that you still find him sexually attractive. This is also the "dangerous age" for a man during which he is likely to pursue a younger woman if only to prove he can still be sexually attractive. It is a critical period in which a warm, sympathetic, supportive, and sensual wife can be the most help to her husband. When he asks the inevitable, "Is this all there is?" she can provide reassurance that what there is isn't bad. When he frets about losing his hair and gaining a paunch, or when he's depressed and discontented, she can make him feel that he's pretty terrific. If she helps him to a greater acceptance of himself, the "dangerous age" can be a time of renewed intimacy, sharing, and growth.

Fundamentally, in order to enjoy the golden years of your honeymoon, you must stop deprecating or diminishing yourself. Life diminishes those who diminish themselves. Any rigid form of self-definition is limiting. A person who labels herself or himself, and then says, "I've got to be me," usually doesn't have much of a "me" to be. Persons who believe in their potential for growth are the ones who set goals that enable them to become better.

Austen to Zola

If "the best is yet to be," you have to rid yourself of definitions and limitations, including those having to do with age. Think of yourself as a composite of strengths and weaknesses, virtues and vices, energy and enervation, most of which have little to do with how many years you've been alive. There is no appropriate age for endeavor or for emotion, and absolutely no time limit exists on creativity. You can run at any age—as the millions of senior joggers out on our highways are doing. You can fall in love as easily at 60 as at 16. And as for being creative, some of the greatest achievements in the arts and sciences, some of the biggest business successes, have been made by persons who might, if they chose, have considered themselves too old.

If you decide that you *can* do something, you're well along the road to doing it. This goes double when we're talking about a wife and husband, for their energies support and reinforce each other.

You must avoid enshrining sex as a goal. When a couple grows older, they're both wise enough to know that the sex act doesn't have to be compulsive or frantic—you're in bed, not on the Hindenburg five minutes after fire broke out. Truly sensual people don't feel they have to be ready to have sex on demand at any time, their clocks are not always set at sex o'clock, and neither feels the necessity to deliver as regularly as the postman. The emotional aura of a marriage is far more important, and a sensual attitude emanates tenderness, sensitivity, and *caring*—even when a couple isn't Going All the Way.

One retired couple decided to indulge their favorite hobby of reading to each other, but with a more concentrated purpose. No more haphazard or random reading. They were going to go right through the world's great masterpieces of fiction, from Jane Austen to Emile Zola. They spent a month just making up their list, choosing 41 English, 24 American, 18 French, 9 Russian, 4 German, and one novel each from Spanish, Polish, Swedish, and Brazilian literature. Then they embarked on what they said was "the great adventure" of their married lives.

They now conduct a seminar in their community. And they're planning a booklovers' tour to England next summer to visit the sites of famous novels and the homes of famous authors. That would never have happened if they hadn't embarked on their reading project.

Your approach, of course, needn't be as disciplined as theirs. You can catch your pleasures on the wing. But every experience you greet with open arms is likely to return your embrace.

Life, That Magician

After 24 years as an actress and 19 as the wife of Paul Newman, Joanne Woodward felt that she was caught in a no-woman's land between the generations. "I was raised to believe that a woman's true fulfillment is in being a wife and mistress to her husband, and a mother to her children. Now the word is that you're a failure if you're nearing 50 and not thin, desirable, vital, doing your own thing, and also having an absolutely terrific sex life." The effort of trying to balance all the demands on her led to an emotional conflict in which she felt like a "displaced person." She was unable to comfort herself with the fact that she was a famous actress in her own right, successfully married to a super star, mother and stepmother to six children, active in the Planned Parenthood movement, a fine cook, an accomplished needleworker, an opera and a ballet buff and, in Paul Newman's opinion, "one of the last of the really great broads."

Joanne was so depressed that she didn't even think she could act any more—although, she told herself, "I must. If I don't I'll become really impossible!" But she dropped out of a role with the Lincoln Center Repertory Theater because she didn't feel equal to it.

At this low stage in her emotional life, another husband might have suggested that she needed professional help. But Paul Newman—who happens to be one of the last of the really great husbands—encouraged her to take a role in a movie. While she was explaining why she couldn't and what a failure she was, he simply looked her in the eye and told her to cheer up.

"What have I got to be cheerful about?" she asked.

"You have a great figure and you make a hell of a hollandaise sauce," he answered.

Joanne took the movie role after all. Her performance was hailed as "masterly" and won her an Academy Award nomination. Today, whenever Joanne starts to feel sorry for herself, she still thinks back to that incident and feels better because, "You know? He's *right!*"

You, too, can turn a feeling of discouragement into triumph if you keep a sense of perspective and an open attitude toward what life may bring.

A couple we know, Joan and Richard, for many years rented a summer house in East Hampton, Long Island. One year the house they had always rented was sold, and it was too late to find another suitable house within their price range. Did they bemoan their bad luck or give up in discouragement? They did not.

Since they live in Manhattan, they decided to find out for themselves whether there was anything to the slogan that proclaims *New York City Is A Summer Festival*. They went to all the Broadway plays they wanted to see, dined in all the fabulous restaurants they'd always intended to try, and toured the city like sightseers—taking the Circle Line boat around Manhattan, visiting the Statue of Liberty, the Empire State building, even Edgar Allan Poe's cottage. All of this didn't come close to equaling the cost of renting their beach house. Furthermore, Richard didn't have to commute for the long weekends, which meant they were able to spend much more time together.

"It was the best summer we ever had," Joan says.

"And there was an entirely unexpected benefit. One night we gave a big party for all our married 'bachelor' friends whose wives and families were away for the summer. One man brought a guest, who happened to be a big shot in an advertising agency. He liked Richard, and they met for lunch. Richard was offered a better job at a better salary. Now, who could have predicted that?"

No one could predict it, and that unpredictableness is one of the best reasons for keeping your options open. Life, that magician, has more tricks up its sleeve than any of us can anticipate. Go along with the show—and enjoy yourself!

This may seem to have only a peripheral interest for those who want to know how to avoid a humdrum marriage and how to honeymoon for life. But the secret of happiness in marriage is fundamentally the secret of happiness itself. Open yourself to all the joys of life. Take them in with all your senses.

In the beginning, I said we were going to look for answers together. That kind of search never really ends. But I hope you've learned along the way that there is no reason for your marriage to lapse into "dailiness," and that by making the right kind of effort you can ensure that it never will.

If I had to sum up the principal message of the book in a few words, it would be this: Don't be his wife, be his lover. By now you know I'm not talking solely about sex. As Germaine Greer says, "Nothing is more desolating than mere sexual expertise. A good lover is loving out of bed."

The full, rich, sensual life is within the reach of everyone. You and your husband can be honeymooners—not for a week or those brief youthful years, but for life. And you can begin right now, the instant you put down this book.